THE WORDS OF GARDNER TAYLOR

VOLUME 3

The Words of Gardner Taylor

(available in both hardcover and paperback)

Volume One
NBC Radio Sermons, 1959–1970

Volume Two
Sermons from the Middle Years, 1970–1980

Volume Three
Quintessential Classics, 1980–Present

Volume Four
Special Occasion and Expository Sermons

Volume Five
Lectures, Essays, and Interviews

Volume Six
50 Years of Timeless Treasures

Available also as a six-volume set.

AUDIO RESOURCES
Essential Taylor and *Essential Taylor II*
    compact disks or audiocassettes
    featuring selections from the multi-volume series

THE WORDS OF GARDNER TAYLOR

VOLUME 3

QUINTESSENTIAL CLASSICS

1980 – Present

Gardner C. Taylor

Compiled by Edward L. Taylor

Judson Press
Valley Forge

The Words of Gardner Taylor, Volume 3: Quintessential Classics, 1980–Present

The sermons "The Answer to a Riddle," "An Appeal to the Hero in Us," "The Authority of Experience," "Balm in Gilead," "Beauty Which Fadeth Not Away," "Chariots Aflame," "God's Promise for Our Temptation," "A Great New Testament 'I AM'," "A Human Request and a Divine Reply," "A Kind Answer to a Sad Question," "The Soul's Desperate Plea," "Spiritual Success," and "Struggling but Not Losing" appeared in *Chariots Aflame* by Gardner Taylor (Nashville: Broadman Press, 1988). Copyright by Gardner C. Taylor.

"The Beautiful People" first appeared in *Pulpit Digest,* January–March 2000, 123–28, published by Logos Productions Inc. Reprinted by permission of the publisher.

Unless otherwise noted, Bible quotations in this volume are from *The Holy Bible,* King James Version. Other quotations are from The Revised Standard Version (RSV) of the Bible, copyright © 1946, 1952, and 1971, by the Division of Christian Education of the National Council of Churches of Christ in the U.S.A. Used by permission. *The New Testament in Modern English* (Phillips), Rev. Ed. Copyright © J. B. Phillips 1972. Used by permission of The Macmillan Company and Geoffrey Bles, Ltd.

Library of Congress Cataloging-in-Publication Data
Taylor, Gardner C.
  The words of Gardner Taylor / Gardner C. Taylor ; compiled by Edward L. Taylor.
    p. cm.
    Includes bibliographical references.
    Contents: v. 1. NBC radio sermons, 1959–1970. ISBN 0-8170-1466-7
(paperback : alk. paper). v. 2. Sermons from the Middle Years, 1970–1980.
    ISBN 0-8170-1467-5 (paperback : alk. paper). v. 3. Quintessential classics, 1980–Present. ISBN 0-8170-1468-3 (paperback : alk. paper). v. 4 Special occasion and expository sermons. ISBN 0-8170-1469-1 (paperback : alk. paper). v. 5. Lectures, essays, and interviews. ISBN 0-8170-1470-5 (paperback : alk. paper). v. 6. 50 years of timeless treasures. ISBN 0-8170-1471-3 (paperback : alk. paper).
    1. Baptists Sermons. 2. Sermons, American. I. Taylor, Edward L.
II. Title
BX6452.T39 1999
252'.061 – dc21   99-23027

Printed in the U.S.A.
09   08   07   06   05   04
10   9   8   7   6   5   4   3   2   1

To Dr. Ruby Taylor Harris,
cousin and counselor,
with happy memories of our childhood
and hallowed memories of our elders
who wait for us now in the Father's House

CONTENTS

PREFACE   xi

ACKNOWLEDGMENTS   xiii

Introduction
GARDNER C. TAYLOR:
AMERICA'S TWENTIETH-CENTURY PREACHER   1

1. THE ANSWER TO A RIDDLE
   (John 14:12–13)   11

2. AN APPEAL TO THE HERO IN US
   (Matthew 9:9)   17

3. THE AUTHORITY OF EXPERIENCE
   (John 9:25)   23

4. BALM IN GILEAD
   (Jeremiah 8:22)   29

5. THE BEAUTIFUL PEOPLE
   (John 17:22)   35

6. BEAUTY WHICH FADETH NOT AWAY
   (Psalm 90:17)   41

7. BEING GLAD ABOUT BEING A CHRISTIAN
   (Mark 2:18–19)   47

8. BELIEVING AND SEEING
   (John 11:40)   52

9. BRIGHT SONGS IN DARK NIGHTS
   (Job 35:10)   56

10. Wide Visions from a Narrow Window
    (Job 19:25–27)   64

11. Chariots Aflame
    (Joshua 17:18; 2 Kings 6:17)   70

12. A Christian Plan for Living
    (Philippians 3:13–14)   75

13. The Christian Response to Trouble
    (Acts 8:4)   81

14. A City with Other Walls
    (Zechariah 2:3–5)   87

15. Enough God
    (Mark 4:37–39)   92

16. The Everywhereness of God
    (Psalm 139:7–8)   99

17. God's Promise for Our Temptations
    (1 Corinthians 10:12–13)   105

18. A Great New Testament "I Am"
    (John 10:9)   110

19. His Own Clothes
    (Mark 15:20)   116

20. How Not to Faint
    (Luke 18:1)   122

21. A Human Request and a Divine Reply
    (John 14:8–9)   128

22. The Key to It All
    (John 21:15–17)   134

23. A KIND ANSWER AND A SAD QUESTION
    (Luke 17:12–17)   142

24. PRAYER OF THANKSGIVING
    (Habakkuk 3:2)   148

25. THE SONG OF MOSES AND THE SONG OF THE LAMB
    (Exodus 15:2–3,7; Revelation 15:1–3)   155

26. THE SOUL'S DESPERATE PLEA
    (Psalm 19)   163

27. SPIRITUAL SUCCESS
    (Psalm 16:8)   168

28. A STORM-PROOF RELIGION
    (Matthew 8:23–27; Mark 4:35–41)   174

29. STRUGGLING BUT NOT LOSING
    (2 Corinthians 4:8–10)   182

30. THREE DAYS THAT CHANGED THE WORLD
    (1 Corinthians 15:3–4)   188

31. THREE WOMEN AND GOD
    (The Book of Ruth)   195

32. WHAT "BORN AGAIN" REALLY MEANS
    (John 3:3)   202

About the Author

Dr. Gardner Calvin Taylor is presently pastor emeritus of the historic Concord Baptist Church in Brooklyn, New York, where he served as pastor from 1948 to 1990. Dr. Taylor has been widely acclaimed as one of the most outstanding preachers in the nation. He has preached on six continents, delivered the 100th Lyman Beecher Lectures at Yale University, and preached the sermon at the prayer service for the inauguration of President William Jefferson Clinton in 1993.

Now retired from the pastorate, Dr. Taylor continues to be in great demand as a preacher and lecturer. He recently accepted an appointment as distinguished professor of preaching at New York Theological Seminary. Dr. Taylor lives in Brooklyn, New York, with his bride, Phillis Taylor.

About the Compiler

Edward L. Taylor is founding pastor of the New Horizon Baptist Church in Princeton, New Jersey. During his ten years of ordained ministry, he has preached at colleges and universities across America and has ministered in Europe, the Caribbean, and Africa. Rev. Taylor has received numerous citations and awards for preaching and congregational ministry. He presently serves as a dean of Christian education for the General Baptist Convention of New Jersey.

A native of Ville Platte, Louisiana, Rev. Taylor currently resides in New Jersey with his wife, Constance La Trice Taylor, and infant son, Paul Lewis Taylor.

PREFACE

Crowds began to form the throng of parishioners making their way into Mount Zion Baptist Church of Alexandria, Louisiana. As I paced toward the church's rear entrance, currents of anticipation could be felt emanating from the people who walked by my friends and me; Louisiana had come to hear her native son — Gardner Calvin Taylor.

We sat in a crowd numbering nearly one thousand, hearing music and testimonies. Many of Dr. Taylor's college friends shared tales about his student years. The congregation seemed pleased to hear stories about the seasoned saint who was about to stand. As friends spoke, Dr. Taylor quickly slipped his glasses on and off, sizing up the congregation.

After the hymn, Dr. Taylor stood, drawing the audience into his homiletic grasp. At his jokes we laughed. By his wit we were charmed. Before we knew it, we were in his hands as he spoke his trademarked words, "Now let me seek my footing in the Word of God." The audience drew near as Dr. Taylor read, "Who is God our Maker who gives us songs in the night?" (Job 35:10). That very sermon, titled "Bright Songs in Dark Nights," appears in this volume.

The sermon captivated those of us in attendance that afternoon in Louisiana. We noted Dr. Taylor's expert craftsmanship. He molded the message for us. It seemed as if we sat at the side of Job himself. I thought I could hear his moans, groans, and questions. I felt for him. Perhaps many that were present thought of themselves as Job for a few faithful minutes.

That wonderful day in 1992 was the first time I heard Gardner C. Taylor preach in person. As a young preacher, I was enamored by who and what Dr. Taylor represented. He embodied a clergyman to be admired as much for his statesmanship as a denominational leader and church builder as for his preaching. This

Dr. Taylor, whom I first knew before any other, appears within these pages.

This volume represents Dr. Taylor's pulpit work at Concord Baptist Church during the 1980s and 1990s. The sermons collected here reflect the musings of an elder statesman on the gospel — a gospel he has come to know so well. Changes in Dr. Taylor's style through the years are apparent after a serious reading of these sermons in contrast with those messages collected in Volumes 1–2. His increased capacity for brevity of expression without forsaking meaningful content may be noted. Increasingly, his messages became more textual in their intimate relationship between the Scripture and sermon. This relationship will become more conspicuous in the expository sermons to be published in Volume 4 of this series.

Most importantly, this volume contains many of the sermons for which he has come to be known among today's leading preachers and homileticians. These later works are the fruition of Dr. Taylor's years of experience at work within a rich tradition of black preaching. They are a culmination of what has been forged in the fire of human experience and brightened by the radiance and glory of God's glorious Spirit. As you cherish the work and wisdom of Gardner Calvin Taylor, may they cause you to bear fruit in your own labors for the Kingdom.

EDWARD L. TAYLOR

ACKNOWLEDGMENTS

I would like to extend my heartfelt thanks to Judson Press for the opportunity to bring these sermons, addresses, lectures, and other works by Dr. Gardner C. Taylor to the American public. The publisher's skill and objectivity have made the process of publication a joy. The technical assistance provided by Mrs. Phillis Taylor, Pamela Owens, Gloria Arvie, and my wife, Constance La Trice Taylor, along with the contributions of DBS transcription services of Princeton, were invaluable.

A debt of gratitude is owed to the Chicago Sunday Evening Club and to the libraries of Union Theological Seminary of Virginia, Yale University, Harvard University, Howard University, The Southern Baptist Theological Seminary, and the Princeton Theological Seminary for the invaluable resources provided to me for the compiling of this work.

In addition, I must acknowledge with appreciation the work of Deacon Bernard Clapp of the Concord Baptist Church of Brooklyn. Deacon Clapp has worked diligently for twenty-five years as head of Dr. Taylor's tape ministry and provided the bulk of the materials found in these volumes.

Most of all I wish to thank Dr. and Mrs. Taylor for their understanding, patience, and cooperation in this project. How grateful I am to have been afforded the opportunity to compile *The Words of Gardner Taylor*. I thank God for having so gifted Dr. Taylor that we should be given this rich corpus of material.

EDWARD L. TAYLOR

Introduction

GARDNER C. TAYLOR

America's Twentieth-Century Preacher

by Edward L. Taylor

Early in United States history, the names Cotton Mather, Jonathan Edwards, and George Whitefield begin an exclusive list of American preaching legends. Since then, Henry Ward Beecher, John Jasper, Phillips Brooks, Jarena Lee, C. T. Walker, Lacy Kirk Williams, Sojourner Truth, and Harry Emerson Fosdick are among the names to be added to the roster of those who have displayed excellence in preaching. Many others could be included.

One name, however, deserves singular recognition among Americans who have proclaimed the gospel of Jesus Christ. That name is Gardner Calvin Taylor. Rarely do legends live in their own time, but Dr. Taylor has proved to be an exception to the general rule. His preaching stands as an unparalleled model — indeed a lighthouse — for all who would aspire to preach Jesus.

Gardner Taylor was born on June 18, 1918, in Baton Rouge, Louisiana. His father, Washington Monroe Taylor, pastored one of Louisiana's most prestigious churches, the Mt. Zion Baptist Church, which is registered today in the Baton Rouge Courthouse as the First African Baptist Church.

Washington Monroe Taylor, who also served as vice president at large of the National Baptist Convention, U.S.A., died when Gardner was just thirteen years of age. But under the tutelage of his mother, Selina, young Gardner developed into an outstanding student, eventually enrolling at Leland College, a black Baptist college located in Baker, Louisiana, just ten minutes from Baton Rouge.

As a college student, Dr. Taylor displayed a wide range of interests and talents. He was a star center who led his football team to

1

victory against Grambling. He was a serious student who devoted much of his free time to reading books. He excelled in extracurricular activities, especially debate. Among the several classmates he regularly engaged in informal, friendly debates was H. Beecher Hicks Sr. The debates, accounts of which have found their way into Louisiana Baptist lore, typically focused on matters of faith. Dr. Taylor made use of several resources, but his favorite text was Robert Ingersoll's *The Mistakes of Moses.*

During his college years, Dr. Taylor looked to Leland College President Dr. James Allen Bacoats, who succeeded Washington Taylor at Mt. Zion, as his primary mentor. Although surrounded and influenced by ministers his whole life, Dr. Taylor did not at first aspire to become one himself. Instead, he wanted to be a lawyer, and in pursuit of that plan he applied to and was accepted at the University of Michigan School of Law.

A tragic personal experience, however, would change not only his plans for law school but also the entire direction of his life. On a spring night in 1937, Dr. Taylor had taken President Bacoats' car on an errand. On a rural highway, a model-T Ford came out of nowhere and crossed his path. The impact was devastating. Two white men were in the car. One died instantly; another died later as a result of the crash. In those days, the society's instincts were to regard a black nineteen-year-old participant in such an accident as a murderer.

Thankfully, however, at the court hearing, white Southern Baptist minister Jesse Sharkey, a witness to the accident, testified that young Taylor was innocent of any wrongdoing. Freed from any fear of prosecution, Dr. Taylor put aside his letter of acceptance to law school and began to think about the ministry instead. Out of this tragic experience, he ended up thanking God and offering himself to God for a lifetime of service.

In the fall of 1937, Dr. Taylor enrolled at Oberlin Graduate School of Theology. While there he wooed and later (in 1940) won the hand of Laura Scott, his first wife, who now sits with Jesus. During those years, the soon-to-be Mrs. Taylor began sharing with Dr. Taylor her love for literature, plays, food, and other elements of the larger culture that would go on to inform Dr. Taylor's preaching. She began her helpful critiques of his work, critiques that would continue throughout her life. During a period in which Dr. Taylor was heavily involved in politics, she said to him, "Your preaching is getting a little thin." That was all the counsel he needed to cut back on his political involvement.

At Oberlin, Dr. Taylor began several practices that, through the years, have greatly influenced his preaching. Most significantly, he immersed himself in the study of preaching as an academic discipline. Like Andrew Blackwood, he realized that every master preacher he respected had made a study of admired preachers.[1] He read sermons constantly, especially those of such nineteenth-century legends as Alexander Maclaren, F. W. Robertson, Frederick Norwood, Leslie Weatherhead, Clarence Macartney, and Charles Spurgeon. He read preaching journals such as *Christian Century Pulpit* from cover to cover.

When a student of preaching inquired of the great expositor Stephen Olford what the difference was between the pastor in England and the pastor in the United States, Olford stated in quick retort, "The pastor in America has an office. The pastor in England has a study." Defying that stereotype, Gardner Taylor has always had a study.

While still a student at Oberlin, Dr. Taylor became pastor of Bethany Baptist Church in Elyria, Ohio. His first pastoral experience, which ended upon his graduation in 1940, affected him deeply and helped him mature in many ways. Since then, he has always shown great love and sensitivity toward those who are starting out in pastorates or going through times of trial in churches across America.

Upon graduating, Dr. Taylor returned to Louisiana to become pastor at Beulah Baptist in New Orleans. In 1943 he returned to Baton Rouge to become pastor of his home church, Mt. Zion. Just a few years later, he was presented with two rare opportunities, remarkable for a man of just twenty-nine.

The first consisted of an invitation to speak at the six-thousand-member Concord Baptist Church in Brooklyn, New

York, whose pulpit had been recently vacated by the death of Dr. James Adams. To the astonishment of many, Dr. Taylor declined Concord's invitation to preach because it fell on Communion Sunday at Mt. Zion. (Some would consider it divine providence that on the date on which Dr. Taylor was originally invited to preach, New York City was besieged by a major snowstorm, among its worst ever.) To Dr. Taylor's surprise, he was reinvited to preach at Concord, and this time he accepted. On the Sunday he preached, Concord was filled to capacity. The sermon, "I Must Decrease, and God Must Increase," captivated those in attendance.

The second of twenty-nine-year-old Taylor's remarkable opportunities was the chance to travel to Copenhagen, Denmark, to attend the Baptist World Alliance. On the Sunday morning of the Alliance, he preached at Second Baptist Church of Copenhagen. Upon returning from his six-week trip to Denmark, Taylor was informed that Concord had invited him to become its next pastor.

No one who knew Taylor doubted that he would accept the invitation. They perceived him correctly as a man of vision whose mind was energized with great and inspiring thoughts and who possessed an immeasurable hope and desire to contribute to the advancement of the Christian faith. Many pastors move on because God has placed before them the challenge of a larger church. For Dr. Taylor, it was more than that. His response to this call entailed fulfilling his role in the destiny of the kingdom of God. As Dr. Taylor's friend Davis Iles put it, "Gardner was big enough for the field, but the field was not big enough for Gardner."

At the 1948 State Convention in Alexandria, Louisiana, Taylor announced his intention to accept the position at Concord. In doing so, he told delegates, "God has called me to preach at the crossroads of the world. I must go." No one in Baton Rouge had to go far to hear Taylor's farewell sermon at Mt. Zion. Radios throughout the black community were tuned to the church's weekly radio program. According to local seniors, it was as if Dr. Taylor were preaching in every home.

At age thirty, Taylor went north, serving the Concord Church from 1948 to 1990, in the process amassing what is among the most respected pastoral records in the twentieth century. Eleven months into his pastorate, Dr. Taylor began serving on a local school board. He went on to become the second African American to serve on the New York City Board of Education.[2] For a short time, he led the Democratic party in Kings County, America's second most powerful political party organization, behind Mayor Daly's Cook County in Chicago.

Nine thousand people were added during Dr. Taylor's tenure at Concord; the church experienced enormous growth. When the building was destroyed by fire in 1952, Dr. Taylor oversaw the building of its present sanctuary, completed in 1956 at a cost of $1.7 million. He presided over the establishment of the Concord Elementary School, where wife Laura served as principal for thirty-two years at no salary; of the Concord Nursing Home, which was founded with 121 beds, along with a seniors residence; and of the Concord Credit Union that went on to amass assets of $1.8 million. He also helped to establish the Christfund, which was endowed with $1 million to support community development, especially in the area of youth.

Despite these accomplishments, however, it is Dr. Taylor's record as a preacher that has distinguished him in American Christianity. The diversity and sheer number of places where he has spoken are a measure of the respect he has earned as a preacher. He has preached before the Baptist World Alliance on six occasions. He followed Harry Emerson Fosdick and Ralph Stockman on NBC *National Radio Vespers Hour,* which was broadcast on some 100 radio stations. National denominations from ten foreign countries, including China, England, and South Africa, have invited him as a special guest. He has also appeared before eleven U.S. denominations.

Even as an octogenarian, Dr. Taylor continues to receive acclaim and honor for his homiletic skills. He has received nearly 100 honorary degrees. He has served as president of the Progressive National Baptist Convention. A countless number of seminaries and colleges have invited him to preach or lecture. Among them is Yale University, where Dr. Taylor delivered the prestigious Lyman Beecher Lectures. Twice, *Ebony* magazine has honored him as one the greatest preachers in American history. *Newsweek* included an account of Baylor University's distinction of Taylor as one of the twelve greatest preachers in the English-speaking world. In an article on the seven great preachers of the pulpit, *TIME* magazine called him "the Dean of the nation's Black Preachers."[3]

I once asked Dr. Taylor that all-important question, "Are great preachers born or made?" After considering for a brief moment, he remarked, "I think that God gives one natural gifts, but there are some secrets. Those may be learned."

One of the underlying secrets to Dr. Taylor's success is simply hard work. He has read thousands of books, most of which now rest in his own library. Nearly every week he wrote a full sermon manuscript over a period of several days. Typically finishing on Saturday, he would then commit its contents to memory. Very rarely does he speak without a manuscript of his remarks on file. Given two years' notice before delivering the Lyman Beecher Lectures at Yale University, Dr. Taylor kept up with his regular preaching and writing schedule, teaching appointments, and pastoral and family duties while still finding time to read all of the previously delivered lectures, which numbered about seventy book-length manuscripts.

In Dr. Taylor's preaching can be found a mix that includes a sort of grand nineteenth-century Victorian style, the richness of the African American folk tradition, and a unique interpretation of modern homiletical theory. The richness of his words and sermon design are legendary. Without fail, his introductions whet the listener's appetite. Like an *hors d'oeuvre,* they hold us for a time but make us eager for more. His message moves toward its purpose as a staircase headed to the top floor of a mansion. His rich language and genius for metaphor help to assure listeners that what may appear to be a steep climb is actually an escalator ride.[4] Each message includes thoughtful theological reflection and biblical scholarship, while steering clear of intellectual arrogance and abstraction. To Dr. Taylor, content and delivery are of equal importance. His delivery contributes to his distinctive interpretation of every text, personifying what Phillips Brooks defined as truth through personality.[5] Dr. Taylor embodies the best of what preachers have been and the hope of what preachers should become.[6]

Hearing Dr. Taylor preach opens a window to the essence of his soul. There we gain a glimpse of how his character has been wedded to the text. His legendary marking of the cross with his foot grounds him. His thumbs behind his lapels lift him as he hangs his head in sorrow with Job at his narrow window, enters the dressing room while a freshly bruised Jesus puts on his own clothes, or bathes himself in the blood which is a balm in Gilead. Such skill is unique in preaching. He exhibits his own prescription for sermon building, displaying genuine pathos and ethos through his mastery of African American rhetoric, through eloquence, and by grasping each audience's understanding of the human circumstance.[7] These are the very qualities that endeared Dr. Taylor to Martin Luther King Jr. and that should endear him to us as well.[8]

Dr. Taylor has proven the adage that "diamonds are made under pressure." Many people with similar gifts have faltered at accepting the challenge to greatness in their professions, but Dr. Taylor rose to the occasion. Each invitation became for him an opportunity to be gifted by God for the experience at hand. In part because of who he is as a person, Dr. Taylor is revered as a preacher among preachers. His ministry has never been clouded by personal scandal. He has a unique reputation for not changing his preaching schedule when invited to larger or more prestigious places. All this helps to explain why fellow clergy have granted him the standing he deserves today.

Although retired for nearly a decade, Dr. Taylor still maintains a hectic schedule, spending time with Martha, the daughter of his first marriage, her family, and his new bride, Mrs. Phillis Taylor. Frequently, he crosses the country preaching in pulpits all over the nation and occasionally overseas as well. He recently accepted an appointment as distinguished professor of preaching at New York Theological Seminary.

I am privileged to have had the opportunity to compile *The Words of Gardner C. Taylor* for the American public and, indeed, for all the world. Most of the sermons in these volumes were first preached in the Concord pulpit. Volume One contains sermons preached on the NBC *National Radio Vespers Hour* in 1959, 1969, and 1970. Future volumes will contain additional sermons (many of which have never before been published), lectures, articles, interviews, presentations, and special addresses, including his Baptist World Alliance addresses, the Martin Luther King Jr. memorial sermon, his address at the funeral of Samuel DeWitt Proctor, and the sermon delivered at the inauguration of United States President William Jefferson Clinton. (Readers should note that some editorial revision by Dr. Taylor may give these sermons or lectures a modern touch in style or language, but the content of the messages has not been changed in any substantive way.)

For half a century, God has used the words of Gardner C. Taylor to shape lives and develop faith. The purpose of these volumes is to help preserve his legacy. The sermons, lectures, and other selections included in this series are far from exhaustive, but they are highly representative. They are intended for readers' enjoyment, but they can also teach and inspire. Most importantly, it is Dr. Taylor's hope that those who encounter his words, even many years after they were preached, will be drawn to a closer and more intimate walk with God.

Recommended Readings

Susan Bond, "To Hear the Angel's Wings: Apocalyptic Language and the Formation of Moral Community with Reference to the Sermons of Gardner C. Taylor." Ph.D. diss., Vanderbilt Divinity School, 1996.

Gerald Thomas, *African American Preaching: The Contribution of Gardner C. Taylor* (New York: Peter Lang, in press).

Notes

1. William H. Willimon and Richard Lischer, eds., *The Concise Encyclopedia of Preaching* (Louisville, Ky.: Westminster John Knox, 1995), 37.

2. Clarence Taylor, *The Black Churches of Brooklyn* (New York: Columbia University Press, 1994), 118.

3. These remarks may be found in *Ebony* (Sept. 1984; Nov. 1997); *Newsweek* (Mar. 1996); and *TIME* (Dec. 31, 1979).

4. Brian K. Blount, *Cultural Interpretation* (Minneapolis: Fortress Press, 1995), 72.

5. Phillips Brooks, *Lectures on Preaching* (New York: E. P. Dutton & Co., 1907), 5.

6. For discussion of the style and content of African American preaching, see Albert J. Raboteau, "The Chanted Sermon," in *A Fire in the Bones: Reflections on African-American Religious History* (Boston: Beacon Press, 1995); Henry H. Mitchell, *The Recovery of Preaching* (San Francisco, Harper and Row, 1977), *Black Preaching* (New York: J. B. Lippincott, 1970), and *Celebration and Experience in Preaching* (Nashville: Abingdon Press, 1990); Evans Crawford, *The Hum: Call and Response in African American Preaching* (Nashville: Abingdon Press, 1995); Frank A. Thomas, *They Like to Never Quit Praisin' God* (Cleveland: United Church Press, 1997); Bettye Collier-Thomas, *Daughters of Thunder* (San Francisco: Jossey-Bass, 1998).

7. Gardner C. Taylor, *How Shall They Preach?* (Elgin: Progressive Convention Press, 1977), 65.

8. Richer Lischer, *The Preacher King: Martin Luther King and the Word That Moved America* (New York: Oxford University Press, 1995), 50–51.

The Answer to a Riddle

John 14:12–13

Verily, verily, I say unto you, He that believeth on me, the works that I do shall he do also; and greater works than these shall he do; because I go unto my Father. And whatsoever ye shall ask in my name, that will I do, that the Father may be glorified in the Son. (John 14:12–13)

The question was whether this subject should read: "The Answer to a Riddle" or "The Answer to a Puzzle." I think there is a difference between a riddle and a puzzle, though the two words are often used interchangeably. To me a puzzle is more mechanical and less demanding of mental exercise. A riddle suggests more strongly that the mind is called on to give the answer. Usually we may feel our way through a puzzle; we must think our way through a riddle.

A riddle asks for the right answer. Every schoolchild has asked riddles of others. One of the most celebrated riddles in all of history is that of the king who promised vast holdings to any man who would answer the riddle "What is it that does not change?" It is a perplexing, saddening truth that all things change, so the king's question was most baffling. Finally, a wise man of the ruler's realm signaled that he had the answer as to what does not change. The court lords and ladies assembled; the king sat on his throne to receive the answer. The wise subject answered the king's riddle: "Change alone does not change." The riddle, which at first seemed to disguise and hide and prevent any answer, actually contained the answer hidden within its bosom. I have looked upon a certain saying of Jesus as a riddle whose answer I did not have.

I first attempted to preach during the summer of 1937. The simplest arithmetic will tell one that over fifty years lie between now and then. The attempt to preach has been constant, almost unceasing. There is no reckoning the number of texts which have been used as the bases for sermons. These texts stretch naturally from the book of Genesis at the beginning of the Bible all of the way through the book of Revelation. There is one passage which I have never dared to use as a text. I believed it is true, but only because I believe devoutly in the integrity of my Lord Jesus and that he would not fool us under any circumstance. The passage to which I refer is not set down in complicated language. The simplest mind can understand what it says. In the fourteenth chapter of John, that supremely consoling and comforting chapter to those who must enter the valley where the dark shadows lie, Jesus is talking. Hear a part of what he says and which always puzzles me: "The works that I do shall he do also; and greater works than these shall he do."

I, for one, have always fallen back from these words. They seem not possible, and yet if they be the word of my Lord, I will trust them. That does not mean that I could dare presume to declare them to a congregation. Think of who said these words, and you will sympathize with anyone who finds them all too vast, too sweeping, and too total to try to explain. This is Jesus talking, whose life made the Old Testament complete and who exposed the heart of God for all to see. This is Jesus talking, who split the centuries in two with all before him backing up and all after him snapping to attention on the other side that he might stand as the completion of the old dispensation and the inaugurator of the new covenant. This, mind you, is Jesus talking, from whom devils ran pleading and crying. Look at the procession of "made-whole," "brought-back," and "second-chance" people who pass by where Jesus has been and whose lives he radically and gloriously altered: Simon and Mary Magdalene, the widow from Nain, men born blind, hustlers and extortioners like Zacchaeus. Then hear Jesus say, "Greater things than these he shall do," and realize the Lord Christ is looking at people like you and me.

No, sir, I was not about to try to preach that until two weeks ago — it all came clear. I had been reading, or seeing, only that part: "Greater works than these shall he do." It was being read out of context. Something goes before these words, and something comes after them. This is no carte blanche passed on to us on our own authority and by our own recognizance. This is no promise dangling out in "midair" to be grabbed like a brass ring on a merry-go-round by anybody who reaches out a hopeful hand. These words are tied in inextricably, indissolubly, and inseparably with Jesus himself. Now read the whole verse: "He that believeth on me, the works that I do shall he do also; and greater works than these shall he do; because I go unto my Father."

This was "good-bye" talk, and the disciples did not like it. The dear Lord was preparing his friends for his death and his physical absence. He was saying to them, "I go away." You who have lost someone you loved deeply, and on whom you leaned heavily, know something of how these people felt with Jesus — their teacher, their friend, and their protector — telling them that he would be leaving them physically. They did not know, understandably, that in going away physically the Lord's presence and power would be even stronger than if he was among them in bodily form. Now, this is a mystery that Christ, in going away from the earth, would be giving his people an even greater good.

Jesus submitted to limitations in being in the flesh. Turn over in your mind what a sacrifice the Son of God made in becoming Jesus of Nazareth. He who was universal localized himself. The main headquarters, so to speak, became a branch office. He could not be both here and there, for in becoming flesh he limited himself to being in only one place at a time. And so Lazarus's sister Martha could say to Jesus when their brother had died, "Lord, if thou hadst been here, my brother hath not died" (John 11:21).

I have never been able to preach from this text because I read only "and greater works than these shall he do." I should have read that right after this startling statement, our Lord said, "Because I go unto my Father." He was saying that for him to depart from us physically, new powers would be turned loose which even he did not have available while in the flesh. More people have been wooed and won, touched and turned, to Christ Jesus by his death and resurrection than anything else he did. We have that, but Jesus did not have that to declare to people, except in prospect. We may take them to Calvary and show them in the Gospels how Jesus died, the innocent for the guilty, the good for the bad, how he offered himself a ransom for many. There he showed once and for all the political risk of being true to God. Jesus did not have his death and resurrection to preach as an accomplished fact. *We have that!*

Let every preacher thank God that he has as a centerpiece of the gospel the death and resurrection of our Lord. Paul knew that there is power in the blood. The apostle thus said to the Corinthians, "I determined not to know anything among you, save Jesus Christ, and him crucified" (1 Corinthians 2:2). No one could know all that is meant when the reference is made to our Lord's death by the words "Without shedding of blood is no remission." Blood does make a difference; blood kin makes a difference. Blood transfusions make a difference. So we Christians have what our Lord did not have: his death and resurrection as accomplished truth to declare to men and women.

He said that in going to his Father we would have greater authority and power. We do have a wider range of authority in his resurrection because Jesus Christ here bodily would be limited, and thus our witness to him would be limited. We could present him only where he was localized, fixed at some one point. And how few could get close to him. Henry Drummond, that saintly figure of another time, has in a vivid and picturesque way, sought to imagine the result of Christ never having left us, how limited he would be and how limited we would be. Suppose Jerusalem were his residence. Surely every Christian would want to see Jesus. Those who could get the money might see Jesus; the others could not even hope. They could not pay the cost of going to Jerusalem to see Jesus. Even those who could pay would have a problem. Every ship that started to the East would be filled with Christian pilgrims, all determined to "see Jesus." Every airplane would be thronged with Christian pilgrims, wanting to get to Jerusalem to "see Jesus." Now, when we landed, there would be millions and millions of people ahead of us. People would camp weeks and months in the hope that they might get close. This word would be *impossible:* "Greater works than these shall he do; because I go unto my Father." We do not have to make a pilgrimage to Jerusalem to see Jesus. We have a greater testimony of our Lord than he had, for he now is everywhere. Christ is equally in Brooklyn and in Budapest, equally in San Francisco and in Savannah, equally in Lagos and Louisville. We may worship him here while other Christians anywhere and everywhere may know his presence at the same time.

"Greater works than these shall he do; because I go unto my Father." Look at the results; behold the truth of what the Lord of truth said. Jesus in his days in the flesh healed but a few people; look at how many have been healed by the hospitals he has inspired and the medical knowledge which was preserved and enhanced in his name in the Christian monasteries of the Dark Ages. While our Lord was here in the limitation and humiliation of human body, he never preached beyond Palestine. By his resurrection power, his disciples have been able to preach him from Palestine through Asia Minor, across to Athens and Corinth, to Rome, throughout Europe, Asia, Africa, North America, and South America. In his name, old evils have been faced, pagan customs have been overthrown, foul governments have fallen, and millions upon millions who sat in darkness have seen the great light.

Nor is it over. Greater works yet shall Christ's people do. The best days are not in the past. "Greater works than these shall he do." The force and fire of Christ Jesus do not belong in any past, recent or remote. "Greater works than these shall he do." The mightiest preaching of the dear risen Lord has not yet been heard, the most moving music has not been sung, and the most powerful and prevailing prayers have not yet been prayed. "Greater works than these shall he do." Our highest peak of Christian believing has not yet been attained, our holiest state of grace has not yet been reached, our dearest communion with God has not yet been experienced, our fullest vision of God has not yet been beheld, and our noblest service to the slain and risen Savior has not yet been rendered.

"Because I go unto my Father." How glad must every Christian be that Christ ascended on high and sat down at the right hand of God. We have a friend at court; Christ is gone unto his Father and has sat down on the right hand of God. He ever makes intercession. We may call on him, for he says, "Whatsoever ye shall ask in my name, that will I do." He can do: he sits at the right hand of God. He can help in our needy hour, for he sits at God's right hand. He can heal us when we ask, for he is at God's right hand. We have but to ask him, to call him, to talk to him, and to plead with him, for he is at the right hand of the Father.

~ 2 ~

AN APPEAL TO THE HERO IN US

Matthew 9:9

And as Jesus passed forth from thence, he saw a man, named Matthew, sitting at the receipt of custom: and he saith unto him, Follow me. And he arose, and followed him. (Matthew 9:9)

Parents are first vexed and then pleased with their children. This is the warp and woof, the lengthwise and cross threads of the fabric, the cloth of parental feeling toward children. There are many times in the rearing of a child when two almost opposite thoughts or words will follow one another very quickly. "You little angel" is an expression that comes to mind in a child's actions as one sees something so pure and selfless in a little one's actions. "You little devil" may follow very soon as one sees a streak of ugliness in the child's makeup.

This is a parable of life: we humans are queer mixtures of angels and devils, all housed in the same dwelling place. The same human being has the capacity to make almost any sacrifice, even life, and on the other hand to be so selfishly grasping that he or she seems like a monster in human form. It happens over and over again that some person will commit a heinous and unbelievable crime which revolts the senses of the community. Almost as often, newspaper reporters and television people will ask the offender's neighbors what kind of person he or she is. Time after time, neighbors will express shock, saying, "He or she seemed to be such a nice person — quiet, kind, never harming anybody." The answer to that? We are a weird mixture of what is lofty and what is low.

Most of us are battlefields within. Anne Frank in *The Diary of Anne Frank* spoke for most of us when she said, "The trouble with me is that I am more than one Anne Frank." Even more direct was Paul's anguished howl of pain in Romans: "The good that I would, I do not: but the evil which I would not, that I do.... O wretched [so split, inwardly clashing] man that I am! who shall deliver me from the body of this death [from this warfare, this pain]?" (7:19,24).

We are weird mixtures of angel and devil, decency and filthiness, coward and hero. Now, there are those always around who will appeal to what is lowest and most unlovely in us. And, of course, they have a hearing, and they win converts. All too often our political campaigns degenerate into exploitation of what is ignoble in the American makeup, manufacturing villains, creating enemies, courting old fears and resentments of race, color, section, and class. Much of what we see on the movie and television screen is a reaching for what is lowest in us: violence and sex turned into something cheap and vulgar. There are those bidding for a following among deprived people who play upon the lowest hatreds, angers, frustrations, and a violence proneness found in all oppressed people. Our great advertising industry shamelessly addresses itself to something low in us which makes us desire to be better than our neighbors, to be one step ahead. Well, we preachers are often no better, maybe worse, because the more precious an affection and practice, the uglier is the using of it for base, degraded ends. Preachers who use the religious faith of people for their own unfair and disproportionate greed are harlots and reprobates. God, deliver us from that! So much around us, so many among us, appeal to what is low in us.

Jesus appealed to the hero in us, to what is noble, grand, and royal in the human spirit. He appealed in short to the godlikeness in us, not to the devil in us. I am always jealous of my Lord's right to be looked upon as one who saw life steadily and saw it whole, who really did know what is in humanity, as the Scriptures say. More than once we read, "He knew their thoughts" (Luke 6:8). I am very jealous for that and so rush along to say that our Lord's appeal to the hero in us was not based upon some fuzzy, romantic idealism about how fine and wonderful people are. He lived in no hazy, fantasy world. He spoke sometimes in biting epithets of what was low and base in people. "Whited sepulchres," painted graves, he said of some (Matthew 23:27): all pure and painted on the outside but containing the rotting flesh and whitening bones of dead people. Our Lord saw piercingly into human nature in all of its degradation and sinfulness. He said bluntly, almost cruelly, to a woman at Jacob's well, "The man you are living with now is not your husband" (John 4:17–18, author's paraphrase). Yes, he saw us for what we are in our lowness, foulness, filth, and devilry.

Ah! God be thanked! Jesus saw something else in us grand and splendid, godlike, at the very least, capable of godliness. He appealed not to what was low, cringing, and cowardly in us. He appealed to the hero in our humanity. So it happened on a day when Jesus passed through Capernaum sweeping along on his grand campaign of spiritual conquest and lordship from Bethlehem to Calvary and on to Coronation.

There sat a publican, gathering tax for the hated Romans. No job in Israel was looked upon with so much contempt by Jews as that of tax collector. Mainly, the revulsion and scorn sprang from the fact that the tax gatherer, the publican, was in a business arrangement with a foreign conqueror at the expense of his own countrymen. He was really a toll gatherer, collecting tolls from those who transported property from one place to another. This job was done by private contract, and the contractor would hire others who actually did the work. Having paid the Romans for the right to collect the tax, the contractor got a percentage of the "take." Naturally, as in America, for slickers did not just get started when we were born, those who collected the tax for the foreigner squeezed every bit of extra percentage they could get, skimmed as much cream off the top, as they say, as they could. People hated and despised those publicans. They were seen as "bloodsuckers" of helpless people. "Dirty traitors," Jews would hiss at publicans as they passed them. You will know something of the feeling from the words *Uncle Tom, cat's-paw,* and *stool pigeon.*

There sat Matthew — hated, despised, and perhaps despising himself. Nobody else saw anything at all decent in Matthew as he grabbed his filthy profits, but Jesus did. Everyone else saw only a fallen creature, too low and despicable to be called a man or addressed with any respect. Jesus saw something splendid, though all covered over with layers of loathsomeness. But still underneath, something worthwhile warranted the Lord's interest and his trust.

This is what makes Jesus so precious to some of us. Where others only see trash, he sees something in us worth his attention and worth his confidence. Sometimes people we call important look at us and never seem to see us, not really. A man in Detroit told me some years ago of talking with one of the most famous men of our time. There was a touch of bitterness in his remembrance of that conversation. He said of the famous man, "I don't think he ever really looked at me or heard anything I said." Someone else recalls how at a reception, for instance, one is face-to-face for a moment with someone of wide reputation. The great one "yawns or fidgets and does not try to conceal that the other is unbelievably dull and uninteresting. All the while his eyes are wandering around looking for someone really worth his attention while he tries as politely as possible to pay no attention to what is being said."

Not so with Jesus. No one else saw anything worthwhile in Matthew, but Jesus did. He stopped on his grand march toward a world's redemption and dealt with Matthew, despised Matthew. He said to this contemptible piece of humanity, "Follow me."

The Lord looks on each one of you that way, on each of us. If you were to ask some of us why is it we love the Lord so, I think we could think of many grand and lofty answers. Surely, at the head would be Calvary, that he died for us all. For many of us right next to that, maybe really a part of it, would be the answer, "The Lord saw something in me. He stopped and dealt with me. He cared. He believed that there was something in me that would respond to his grand command and invitation, 'Follow me.' "

Here we are with our small talents and smaller character, and here is the great Lord Jesus, the Lord of glory, mind you, taking an interest in you and me! Mind you, the Object of angels' praise, the Hope of glory, Calvary's Hero, says, "Follow me. I need you. I think you'll make a soldier. Follow me."

Matthew did not ask where the road would lead. Jesus knew that there was something slumbering in Matthew which needed to be awakened. And where the road led was not really the most important matter. What was most important was the question of *who* was leading, not *where* the way was leading. Something dissatisfied in Matthew could be satisfied if he followed the Lord. Matthew knew that. The Scripture suggests that without waiting, flinging his counter and the coins out in the road, Matthew got up and followed.

Any Christian could tell you where the way led for Matthew and how fared the traveler. It is a way for heroes, fighting, forging ahead, falling, rising, forgiving, forgetting, finding that the way grows brighter every passing day.

Following the King — that's what it's all about! There are dangers, but, my God, what thrills, what joy! There will be many who will gladly tell you that Jesus is a mighty good leader. You are safe in following him. "Is it a hard way?" you ask. Oh yes, the road is mighty rocky sometimes, but he smooths out the rocky way as you travel, or he gives you the strength to pass triumphantly through the hard places. "Are there enemies on this way?" you ask. Oh yes, but the Lord who is our leader prepares a table before us in the presence of our enemies. "Do we get weary?" you want to know. Oh yes, but the Lord who is our guide leads by still waters and green pastures. He restores the soul.

The Lord is a mighty good leader. I am so glad that he passed my way in the cane country long ago and offered me a place in his ranks. He is a mighty good leader — or as G. A. Young once wrote:

> Sometimes on the mount
>   where the sun shines so Bright,
> Sometimes in the valley, in darkest of night,
> God leads His dear children along.

Do you not plan to go on, to go on to see what the end will be? For some it has been a long way he has led us, but we know that

If [we] walk in the pathway of duty,
If [we] work till the close of the day;
[We] shall see the Great King in His beauty
When [we've] gone the last mile of the way.

When [we've] gone the last mile of the way,
[We] will rest at the close of the day,
And [we] know there are joys that await [us]
When [we've] gone the last mile of the way.

∾ 3 ∾

THE AUTHORITY OF EXPERIENCE

John 9:25

He answered and said, Whether he be a sinner or no, I know not: one thing I know, that, whereas I was blind, now I see. (John 9:25)

Some years ago I shared a series of lectures and sermons in Florida with my Brooklyn colleague Dr. Harry Wright, the Cornerstone Church preacher. On our last morning together, Dr. Wright spoke with memorable pithiness of the event from the story of the man born blind. I think I shall never forget his piercing insight that Jesus led the blind man in the account from eyesight to insight. Dr. Wright concluded on the high note that the world needs experience's testimony about the goodness of God and the love of Jesus Christ shed abroad in our hearts.

He was right. There are those who like to spin fine theories of God's relationship to us. Many of us like to quote what others have said as to how God has dealt in their lives. And this is good and helpful, but it is not the most forceful form of Christian witnessing. There may be a note of authority which belongs to someone who is able to refer to bright examples in the past of how the Lord has delivered his people and how Jesus Christ has saved men and women from the power of sin. But this is not the highest authority.

The account from John 9 is one of the well-known events reported from the life and public ministry of our Lord Christ. Jesus was moving on his way, the most momentous and far-reaching path ever trodden on the face of the earth. It was the way from Bethlehem to Calvary, a life journey of nearly thirty-three years. All of us who are moving irresistibly and without interruption on our way through life will catch the meaning underneath the words which say, "And as Jesus passed by" (v. 1). Mightn't a

23

preacher gloriously halt right there and thrill to the significance of the Lord passing where we are? The story moves on its way by indicating that a man born blind claimed the attention of the Lord as he passed on his way. The Master stopped, mixed spit with mud, rubbed it on the man's eyes, and commanded the man to go wash in the pool of Siloam. Miraculously, so the record states, the blind man received his sight while his neighbors marveled at the unspeakable deliverance which had come upon him. At this juncture in the account, the Pharisees, the constant opponents of Jesus, begin a running attack on what had happened. Finally, having been questioned and badgered as long as he could bear about his cure, the man who had received his sight took his stand and rested his authority on the experience which he had for himself: "One thing I know, that, whereas I was blind, now I see."

There are many features about this event which cry out for the preacher's attention. Those who make a study of such things tell us that we have some six instances of blindness given to us in the New Testament, but this is the only case where a man was *born* blind. Others remind us that in John's Gospel there are eight miracles recorded, and in all of them except one, the Lord showed his mercy without being asked.

An intriguing question is raised about this man later to be healed by Jesus. The disciples raised the old question which the book of Job should have settled forever. Speaking of this man's affliction, the disciples asked Jesus, "Who sinned, this man, or his parents?" It is the smallest, narrowest, cheapest religion which tries always to make God spiteful, vengeful, and every affliction the result of wrongdoing. Now, with a shudder we must remember that wrongdoing brings its own punishment, inner or outer. God does not have to do that!

Jesus gave the answer which should have dismissed forever this garbled kind of thinking about God and us. Said Jesus with that characteristic graciousness of his: "Neither hath this man sinned, nor his parents" (v. 3). Then our Lord declares a loftier possibility which hangs on every affliction, on every sorrow, and on every disappointment. Jesus added, "But that the works of God should be made manifest in him." And we have seen that. I think of more than one treasured sightless Christian who has confronted with great courage this condition which John Milton described in his blindness as "that one talent which is death to hide, lodg'd with me useless." These of whom I speak have shamed most of us by their bright and cheerful spirit, their steadfast presence in divine worship, and their constant service for others. What a change would come upon the way we look at those things we call our burdens if we saw them as the ways by which the works of God should be made manifest. In other words, our burdens exist to show God's power to lift them. Our sorrows exist to show God's power to comfort. Our hurts exist to show God's power to heal them. Our problems exist to show God's power to solve them. Our sins exist to show God's power to cleanse them. Our disappointments exist to show God's power to reappoint. Our deaths — can we say it? — exist to show God's power to raise us unto life eternal.

Three principal characters emerge vividly from the account which we have before us. Dominant, as always wherever he was, is the figure of our Lord Jesus Christ. Two verses suffice to tell what Jesus did, but the result, the consequence of what he did, fills thirty-three verses. We may look upon this incident as a prophecy, since twenty-seven brief pamphlets which we call the New Testament comprise the record we have of his life, death, and resurrection. Who can count the books that have been written about him? I count well more than a thousand on my own bookshelves. All of the libraries in the world could not hold the books written about Jesus since he walked the earth.

Jesus did for the blind man what the blind man could *not* do for himself and then commanded him to do what he *could* do for himself. Jesus opened a pharmacy, a divine drugstore, on the dirty road where he traveled and took his own spit mixed with mud to anoint the man's eyes. This represents one of but two cases we have in the Gospels of Jesus healing by applying such a poultice. Believe me, there was no healing in the mud wet by spit. Believe me, there was no healing in washing in the pool of

Siloam where Jesus sent the man that he might receive his sight. Rather, I am sure, our Lord here cloaked his power in order to accommodate himself to our poor understanding. Perhaps, also, he applied the humble mixture so the blind man's faith might be aroused that something was happening. So by a gradual method the man received his sight.

It is but one step for me to go on to say that much of our having to wait for answers to our prayers is in order to get us set, positioned, braced, and prepared to receive the Savior. God even accommodates himself to our poor, dim understanding. The power is not in the outward symbols but in God's will. It is not the clay — it is Christ who heals. It is not Siloam's waters but the Savior's will which performs the miracle.

The second characters who emerge are the faultfinders who did not see the blessing of the healing but who looked for some fault in the healer. They were negative, critical, carping, and antagonistic. They inquired as to what had happened and only in order to criticize. "This man," they said of Jesus, "is not of God" (v. 16). Others were bolder, suggesting that Jesus was a sinner because he did not observe their ritual laws. They then went to the parents to see if they could find further excuse to express their critical, unfriendly, and faultfinding spirit.

Mark this! Do anything that is good, try to do anything that is uplifting, and as sure as God made green apples, critics will appear on the scene. Twenty things may be right, and they will say not a good word. Let one thing be wrong, and all of their attention is focused upon that one failure. The presence of such a pessimist is always harmful to any great undertaking. Sometimes these ice-water throwers are not even conscious of their defeatist spirit. When our church had burned and we were relocated on Adelphi Street, I remember a man, most prominent in the life of this country, who stood with me in the temporary sanctuary and told me in mournful tones that many people would leave the church under the load. I think he never knew how negative and chilling he was.

Are you a faultfinder? Those stood against the Lord. Habitual faultfinders are almost always against the cause of God. They are forever looking back or looking down. They chill enthusiasm and freeze the flow of effort and interest. I despise Mr. Fear-all and his wife, Mrs. We-Can't, and their daughter, Miss Much-Afraid. I do not like to be around Deacon Faint-Soul, and Reverend We-Will-Fail gets on my nerves. The world needs "bright hearts" and encouragement givers. If you can't speak a good word, shut up, go somewhere, and pray until the Lord gives you faith and hope that "with God all things are possible" (Matthew 19:20). Ask God to bring you to a radiant hopefulness, an authentic Christian optimism, a love for what is high rather than what is low, to make you a viewer of high horizons rather than a gazer at gutters.

The third figure is that of the man into whose life Jesus had come and whose condition, because of the Lord's touch, was made forever different. There is something bright and splendid about any life with which Jesus has had to do. Show me a man or woman who has been with the Lord, and I will show you somebody who has the authority of a mighty experience.

There is no use theorizing about what God can do and cannot do with someone for whom the Lord has done great things. Argue about limitations, debate the impossible, and believers will cry out because of their experience, "God can do anything but fail." Say to the soul which has had an experience of God's deliverance that this or that cannot be done, and that soul must answer, "God is able." You may not be sufficient, and I may not be sufficient for this or that, but God is able. He can bring peace out of confusion, joy out of sorrow, victory out of defeat, day out of darkness, triumph out of tragedy, health out of sickness, sunshine out of the storm, spring out of winter, laughing out of weeping, and holiness out of sin. God is able!

There is authority in experience. This man who received his sight expressed it, and the more we see of him, the better we like him. This man touched by Jesus has a sturdy boldness, an assurance that cannot be bluffed, cannot be browbeaten, and cannot be scorned and scoffed out of court. They said, "Christ is no good," but he said, "He blessed my life." They said, "Jesus is a sinner," but he said, "I do not know whether he is a sinner. You are examining me on matters about which I am not competent. I have not seen the balance books of God as to who is a sinner and who is not. You are dealing with me at a level where I am not an expert. If you will get to my area where I operate with expert knowledge, I can talk with you. One thing I know. Much I do not know, but one thing I do know. Vast areas of intelligence lie beyond my scope, but I am an expert in one area. The Lord did something for me. 'Whereas I was blind, now I see.' He has made a change in me. He has lifted me from 'shades of night to plains of light,...He lifted me!' This I know."

Whether God can build a highway, some of us do not know. We do know that he can make a way where there is no way. Whether medicine is God's business, some of us do not know. We do know we were sick, and it looked like we couldn't get well, and here we are on our feet. Whether God is a long-range planner or not, we cannot say. Some of us know "he brought us from a mighty long way," found us way down and lifted us way up, found us ignorant and sent us to school, found us friendless and put friends all around us, found us naked and clothed us, found us nothing and made something out of us. On this we may speak with authority.

◦ 4 ◦

BALM IN GILEAD

Jeremiah 8:22

Is there no balm in Gilead; is there no physician there? why then is not the health of the daughter of my people recovered? (Jeremiah 8:22)

The title of this sermon stands as I first heard it more than fifty years ago. The yellowed page on which the main points of the sermon were written is still in my possession and will in time go to the Boston University library, where my papers will one day be housed. In my earliest days as a preacher, I copied the main points of the sermon and tried to preach it. It has now been forty and more years since that sermon was heard by a young woman, a recent graduate with highest honors from Oberlin College, who said upon hearing the sermon that she thought she detected promise in the young preacher. It is not for me to say how sound was her judgment on that day long ago as to that young preacher's future. I do know that she has been hearing that preacher ever since. I felt no shame in taking the points of the sermon since the sermon was by a preacher born in 1870 and he was my father. The points of the sermon are still his; the amplification and application of those points belong to my own spiritual pilgrimage through the years.

Jeremiah spoke out of a deep ache caused by the extreme difficulty in which he saw his own people in Israel trapped and suffering. If we know nothing else about the prophet Jeremiah than these words, we would mark him as a person of the most sensitive makeup and as belonging to that rare and wonderful breed of human beings who feel the sorrows and heartbreaks of their fellows and associates as their very own. Few of us are sufficiently tender of soul to enter actually into sufferings other than our own, to feel truly what another feels, or are able, as our American Indians say, to really walk in another's moccasins.

For instance, do you ever feel pain because someone you know does not know the Lord or will not obey him? Across all of these centuries and struggling up out of the entombment of print, the prophet's words drip with inexpressible grief. Do you hear the pain in the two questions with which the prophet concluded the eighth chapter of the book of Jeremiah, "Is there no balm in Gilead; is there no physician there? why then is not the health of the daughter of my people recovered?"

What the prophet saw in old Israel sent him into the deepest mourning and wrung from his heart sorrow and from his eyes copious tears of sympathy. He saw his people trying to play the game of international politics between Egypt and Babylonia. Israel was not called into nationhood to play the old game of power but to be God's people. How sad to see the people of the Lord trying to be something else. Jeremiah saw that the Babylonian king, Nebuchadnezzar, was an instrument in the divine hand, the wicked, pagan means by which God's people would be brought to judgment for their sins. The profound insight of Jeremiah was that in all the give-and-take, the thrust and counterthrust of human struggle and international politics, there is a sickness, a malady, a sinful disease. The affairs of state and the procedures of government prey more times than not on the sins of the people. The persons who would be leaders say, "I will give you more and a way to get ahead of the other fellow." We are subjected again and again to an "us-against-them" mentality. We are manipulated and victimized again and again by appeals which shrewd people make to something sinful in us — our race, class, section, type of work, neighborhood, or education — anything which will drive a wedge between people and divide us into the "outs" and the "ins." Jeremiah saw this in the parties and cliques and schemes of his own time.

There is a disease in our humanity, and the correct name for it is *sin*. Dress it up if you wish. Call it by some polite name if this will make you feel better. Say that what is wrong with us is "cultural lag" if you choose. Say that what is wrong with us is "ignorance," that when we know what is right, we will do what is right. Jeremiah would tell us that this is trifling with a terrible and fatal disease — sin — which destroys the nervous system of conscience and wrecks the power of right thinking. Sad it is that a polite hypocrisy has censored the word *sin* out of decent speech, so it has almost disappeared from our preaching and has dropped out of our religious vocabulary. No wonder Dr. Karl Menninger, the psychiatrist, wrote a book and entitled it *Whatever Became of Sin?* What other word can describe the sickness which brings us to rebellion against God and our best selves, to estrangement, to unfriendly distance from our Source of being, from God, to error, missing the mark in life?

Jeremiah saw in his people the awful symptoms of this dread disease of sin. In the eighth chapter, the prophet listed some of the effects of this fatal malady. The bones of kings, princes, priests, prophets, and citizens shall become as dung, as fertilizer, on the face of the earth (8:1–3). Death shall be chosen in preference to life. The people had slid back with a "perpetual backsliding." They held fast and firmly to lies and deceit. No one repented. People said that they were wise and needed no guidance. Some had introduced false cures which, as Jeremiah said, healed the hurt of the people only slightly. Many confused and deceived by crying, "Peace, peace; when there is no peace" (8:11). People did the worst things and were not ashamed; neither did they "blush" at the most terrible outrages (8:12).

Then near the end of this most mournful of chapters and at the beginning of the next, all of Jeremiah's pent-up sorrows burst the bounds of self-restraint like a river in flood time. The prophet's cry sends a chill through us:

> The harvest is past, the summer is ended, and we are not saved. For the hurt... of my people am I hurt; I am black [or I mourn in sackcloth and ashes]; astonishment hath taken hold on me. Is there no balm in Gilead; is there no physician there? why then is not the health of the daughter of my people recovered? Oh that my head were waters, and mine eyes a fountain of tears, that I might weep day and night for the slain of the daughter of my people! (8:20–9:1)

"Is there no balm in Gilead?" Now, we are told that Jeremiah was referring to a balsam which the ancient physicians found to have almost unbelievable healing power. The Ishmaelites, the Arabian merchants, brought among their cargo in the camel caravans this powerful, aromatic preparation to Israel. It was credited with marvelous cures. This balm from Gilead reached diseases otherwise beyond the power of the ancient doctors. The worst, the most painful, the most dread sicknesses seemed not beyond its reach. So the prophet cried for some spiritual balm in Gilead which would get down to the awful disease at the center of the soul of the people.

There are several qualities we read about this balm from Gilead which suggest to us our Christ Jesus, who is healing for all of our spiritual sickness and distress. The first thing we notice about the balm from Gilead is that it did not grow in Palestine. It came from a land east of Jordan, from Gilead. It had to be brought into the land from elsewhere. No plant grew naturally in Palestine which was as effective as balm from Gilead for the worst and ugliest diseases of its inhabitants.

In the sickness of the soul, there is no earthly balm, no human cure, which will get to the seat of the disease. Sin has no mortal cure. Education makes the sickness of sin more subtle, more deadly. Wealth makes the disease of sin more resourceful, more adroit. Culture makes this sickness more polished, more sophisticated. Prisons make this disease more virulent, more vicious. Recreation makes this sickness of sin more vigorous and more supple. Nothing grown here on earth can take away this disease.

We have a balm that will cure a sin-sick soul, and it was imported from another land. No one on earth could save us. For such a one to come, prophets longed and priests ministered in hope at countless altars. Generations sighed for some such cure. In the fullness of time, when all things were ready, God sent his Son. In Bethlehem of Judea, there arrived on earth one who heals all our disease and takes away the awful sickness of sin. No wonder the angel said, "Thou shalt call his name Jesus: for he shall save his people from their sins" (Matthew 1:21). Christ came here from a great distance that we might be healed. No mere person could save us, but the one who could and does heal us came as a stranger from a long distance. He was born as a stranger in a stable, lived as a stranger without a place to lay his head, and died as a stranger outside the city's gates:

> Hail the heav'n-born Prince of Peace!
> Hail the Sun of righteousness!
> Light and life to all He brings,
> Risen with healing in His wings.
> Mild He lays His glory by,
> Born that man no more may die,
> Born to raise the sons of earth,
> Born to give them second birth.

There was another quality of the balm of Gilead which resembles our Savior Jesus who is healing for the sickness of our souls. We read that the balm tree was not a tree of beauty and attractiveness. It was not a stately tree, nor did it grow large limbs which would grant to it a great beauty. The tree in Gilead from which the healing balm was extracted was a kind of shrub. It would not compare favorably with our huge oaks or fir trees or the mighty and legendary redwoods of California. Its wood was light and gummy, and it was quite incapable of being polished as mahogany can be polished.

The healer of our soul's hurts was not attractive when he came here and is not now attractive to so many. All of you who are hurting with sin right now want to be healed, but we keep looking for pretty, attractive healers. The government cannot heal us, nor itself, with its new deals, fair deals, new frontiers, or new federalisms. Schools cannot heal your soul, churches cannot heal your soul, priests cannot heal your soul, and preachers cannot heal your soul. For those of us who live under the spells of Bethlehem and Calvary, "There is none other name under heaven given among men, whereby we must be saved" (Acts 4:12). Christ has never been attractive by the world's standards, and the prophet spoke well when he said, "He shall grow up before him as a tender plant, and as a root out of a dry ground: he hath no form nor comeliness; and when we shall see him, there is no beauty that we should desire him" (Isaiah 53:2). The world's warped view cannot see beauty in Jesus, but seen by faith he is altogether lovely, the Lily of the Valley, the Rose of Sharon, the bright and Morning Star, and the "Sun of righteousness [risen] with healing in his wings" (Malachi 4:2).

There is one other quality about the not-so-attractive balm tree which made it a far-famed agent in the healing of disease. The medicine of the tree was not in its leaves, as in Madeira leaves, with which some of our old people wrapped us in order to cool fever. The healing medicine of the balm tree was not in the root bark, as some of us were given in sassafras tea. The healing power in the balm tree was in the thick liquid which flowed out of the tree. There was but one way to release that fluid, and that was by cutting and piercing the tree until it bled its healing fluid.

That child born in Bethlehem came from a long distance and was a stranger to the earth he came to save. That child born in Bethlehem was not attractive and still is not glamorous to those bewitched by this world's fading splendors. And that baby born in Bethlehem had to be bruised, like the balm tree, before healing power could pour forth to save a sin-cursed world and sin-sick souls. The little Christ Child came from a long way to be born in Bethlehem; that same baby at Calvary was wounded that the healing of his crimson flow might make us clean forevermore. That baby born in Bethlehem had to be pierced at Calvary. Our balm in Gilead was bruised for our iniquities, wounded for our transgressions, and "with his stripes we are healed" (Isaiah 53:5). There is no one doctrine of Christ's sacrifice for us which fully covers the subject, but standing — or better, kneeling — at Calvary we know that his broken body in some way beyond telling has opened the way to wholeness for our brokenness. We know at levels deeper than reason that by his wounds we are healed, and in his abandonment the way is open for us to be won forever to God. Christ heals our soul's disease, and he is our balm in Gilead. All the ends of the world, hear! Christ heals, heals all, heals sweetly, and heals completely.

~ 5 ~

THE BEAUTIFUL PEOPLE

John 17:22

And the glory which thou gavest me I have given them; that they may be one, even as we are one. (John 17:22)

The term *beautiful people* was originated by society columnists and other watchers of the idle rich who follow the sun from Manhattan to Palm Beach to Monte Carlo, to the French Riviera and the southern coasts of Italy and Spain. They are the people who show up at places where they can be seen to advantage, wearing the latest fashion creations of Gucci, Bill Blass, and Pierre Cardin. They are supposed to be style setters, pace makers for what is smart and "in," as they say.

The rest of us are likely to envy them, their good fortune and big fortunes, and to wish that we could scamper hither and yon as latter-day sun worshipers. If you look behind the sparkle and paint, you are likely to discover something not so beautiful. Many of these people with nothing to hold on to except their appearance are likely to be in a constant, desperate, losing battle against the bulge in the wrong place, the unwelcome wrinkle, the drying skin, the crow's-feet under the eyes, the middle-age paunch in the men. One begins to wonder how beautiful are these people, so many of whom must disappear from sight for drying-out treatments and alcoholism cures. Puffing on marijuana, "grass," they say, to take the ugliness out of it, or "unlabeled cigarettes," as a young man put it to me, they seem anxious, disturbed, trying a little too hard to be merry and happy. One hears with a little surprise that these beautiful people are likely to be sniffing cocaine to get out of some trap of the spirit where they feel pointless, without meaning, like "scape-graces," that is, those who have escaped the means of grace. It may be criminal misuse of the language to call these "beautiful people." Envy them? Pity them!

There is another kind of humanity that many might call the beautiful people. I point to the power brokers in industry and government. How are they referred to? "Captains of industry," "well-known political figures," are some of the designations. Now, government and great corporations are not evil of themselves, though sometimes they seem close to being that. One does not have to get very close to these people in order to sense that these filmed and written-about folk seem jumpy and nervous. Word keeps leaking out that every junior executive is clawing at the next fellow in order to take his place. I know for a fact you will hardly find a more insecure, uneasy, jumpy group of people than those who hold high public office and who are forever thinking and speaking with one eye on the next election. Along this line, can you imagine a nation with hydrogen bombs, guided missiles, a highly equipped air force, battleships, transcontinental attack weapons, and selective target bombs afraid of every small despot? If nervous is beautiful, then they are beautiful.

We thought once that leaders of minority communities and great religious denominations were powerful and, in a sense, beautiful people — if by that designation we mean "prominence" and "popularity." We discover to our sadness that many of them are self-promoters of the most shameless and reprehensible quality. Far from sacrifice of self in the name of lifting fallen humanity, so the saying once went, they are far more interested in their own welfare and wealth. They mouth the names of our truly great figures like Martin King, but their agendas are far more constricted, being defined by self-centeredness and the unconscionable adventurism of victimizing the masses, themselves all too willing to be hoodwinked and bilked.

Aiding and abetting the pretense of attractiveness are some of our modern inventions, of themselves bearers of incalculable benefits to our humanity. Computers, e-mail, fax machines, and the like are potentially wonderful aids to daily living. Alas! There are two thousand Web sites of bigotry on our computers, according to the Wiesenthal Center in Los Angeles. The most violent and shocking games are peddled to our children, to say nothing of pornography of the most graphic and revolting kind which is readily available to immature minds, juvenile and adult. People so entrapped find it impossible to be beautiful in spirit. Lacking inner attractiveness, they cannot avoid becoming externally repulsive and hideous.

To all of this our Lord Jesus would address a word loaded with godly sorrow as recorded in Mark 6:34: "And Jesus when he came out, saw much people, and was moved with compassion toward them, because they were as sheep not having a shepherd."

What shall we say of those who hold the places of public notice and who head organizations in minority communities? We thought they were beautiful people. We are now being treated to the disquieting spectacle of personal rivalries, insecurities, lust for public notice, being paraded by representative minority people through the avenue of any form of public communication available. When will we learn to differ intensely and vigorously over issues but not to make public attacks on each other's integrity and honor and purpose? No, in all of this I do not see beautiful people, those to be admired, supported. I see immaturity, childishness, anxiety, insecurity, self-centeredness, near-sightedness. Pity and shame! And the masses of minority people who must work day by day with other Americans, and sometimes for them, are again the victims. The word of Jesus previously cited haunts us still: "And Jesus when he came out, saw much people, and was moved with compassion toward them, because they were as sheep not having a shepherd."

There is the illusion abroad that life can be made beautiful by the common sense of men and women, by planning, long and short range. This notion has its roots in a large confidence about the essential goodness of human beings, our perfectibility, our capacity to make ourselves what we want to be. William Henley spoke for this belief in "Invictus" when he cried, "I am the master of my fate; / I am the captain of my soul." Indeed! Henley's last years were a descent into sadness at the death of his daughter and the public anger at his slashing attack on his former friend Robert Louis Stevenson. While we can all make ourselves better people,

we cannot make ourselves beautiful people. Life is too harsh, and
its sorrows too real and too certain. Sin soils and sours our lives
and our relationships, sickness takes the blush off our days, and
death delivers the final, fatal blow.

We cannot make ourselves beautiful, but the Lord can grant
us his beauty. The psalmist perceived that before Jesus placed his
imprimatur on the truth. Such was the parting music of the stately
hymn we call the ninetieth psalm, "Let the beauty of the LORD
our God be upon us: and establish thou the work of our hands
upon us; yea, the work of our hands establish thou it."

The people of Jesus were granted the beauty of his glory, so
says the seventeenth chapter of John. It bears remembering that no
person of sensitive spirit ought to be able to enter the thirteenth
chapter of John and pass through chapter 17 without a pull at the
heartstrings. In these chapters our heads are naturally bowed, our
voices lowered, and our footsteps are quiet. A holiness, a sanctity,
a grand and purposeful sorrow, an inexpressible love, are all to be
seen in these chapters. As we come to chapter 17, we pass through
a holy court where the Calvary-bound Savior has been talking to
his disciples and friends for the last time around their final meal
together. We pass in chapter 17 into the Holy of Holies, where the
Savior, soon to die, turns from earthly conversation to address his
Father in heaven, "Jesus lifted up his eyes to heaven."

During that hallowed discourse, that divine exchange between
the Father in heaven and the Son on earth, we come upon my
text. It is a part of that passage which formed my funeral text for
my fallen colleague Sandy Ray, that marvelously gifted preacher,
"Father, I will that they also, whom thou hast given me, be with
me where I am; that they may behold my glory." Now shortly
before those words are these: "And the glory which thou gavest
me I have given them; that they may be one, even as we are one."
The "glory" refers here to the divine character shedding its bril-
liant glow far out toward all who will look upon it. The honor,
the dignity of God, his grace and power, these comprise the glory
of God, the luminous, warm, bright blessedness of the divine person. And surely here Jesus is talking of his own fleshly life, not

that eternal glory which belonged to him before the morning stars sang together and all the children of God shouted for joy. Does he not pray the glory which "thou gavest me"?

That glory given to the man Christ Jesus, our elder brother, becomes ours by the gift of Jesus. Is it fair and proper to ask as to what are the signs of this glory? How are we to see it? With what body of actuality does it come upon you and me?

Jesus moved in a climate full of the presence of God. He was not first with the Father and then away, in and out. Select one dominant characteristic of the Savior's years on earth, and it would have to be close communion with God. See how often he prayed to the Father. Dr. George Buttrick has told us that Jesus prayed and prayed — talked with God. He prayed in the day's dull routine and in the flaming hour of crisis. He prayed at his baptism. He prayed all night before he chose his disciples. He prayed on the mount of transfiguration. He prayed the High Priestly Prayer here in our text. He prayed in Gethsemane and on Calvary's cross. He prayed until his work was prayer and prayer was his work. His was a constant communion with God. In John's Gospel, he refers to the Father more than one hundred twenty times. Listen and see if you catch some of that theme, some of that drumbeat, that recurring note in some of his words. God the Father provided the bracing climate for his soul. He speaks of himself in the third person, "The Father loveth the Son." Under stress and great and present danger, listen to him; he does not retreat one inch but speaks confidently, "Thinkest thou that I cannot now pray to my Father, and he shall presently give me more than twelve legions of angels" (Matthew 26:53). He is speaking, if you want to be literal and pedestrian, of seventy-two thousand trained angelic warriors. Where are we to go when this is over? Listen to Jesus: "In my Father's house there are many rooms," and at the last, "Father, into thy hands I give my spirit." Jesus moved on earth in the climate of God the Father. This was his theme, his glory, his boast, his trust, his aim, his work, his talk, his breath, his life — God.

The beautiful people, truly beautiful, are those who have been led by Jesus to live in God, to dwell in God. This is our glory! We are not to be visitors but to live in God. We are to talk with him at stated times and unstated times. We ought to have particular times set apart for communing with God, but we ought to commune with him all of the time. Thank God, as we used to sing, "Central's never busy. Always on the line, you may hear from heaven, almost any time. 'Tis a royal service, free for one and all. When you get in trouble, give this royal line a call." Life can be beautiful, its succeeding stages and ages a glory, if we live in God. Stay close to him in sunshine and storm. Beneath the shadow of his throne, his saints forever dwell secure.

Thus close to him, the beauty of the glory of the Lord our God will be upon us. We shall walk in the sunshine of his love. We shall find shelter beneath the shadow of his wings. We shall walk through this valley in peace. We shall be able to smile though all hell rages around us. We shall be able to turn back every enemy, overthrow every idol. We shall walk through the fire, and the fire shall not burn us. We shall pass through the waters, and the waters shall not overflow us. We shall look evil and sickness and sorrow and trouble and tears and great trials in the face and say to them, "My Father is my protection, my shield, my defender, my trust, my hope, my boast."

So Christ gives us the glory that the Father gave him, and we are beautiful in that spiritual privilege. What an amazing gospel! Christ gives to us his glory. He makes us joint heirs. He gives us the full liberty of the children of God. He gives us the key to all the storehouses he possesses. He empties his blessing in our hands. He sets us down at his table and bids us to feast until we want no more.

Rejoice, Christian, rejoice evermore. Let the world know that Christ has taken us in, has put on us his royal robe. He has made us princes and princesses of the house regal, kings and priests unto our God forever, the blessed of his Father. We now own all that Christ has — all of his grace, all of his peace, all of his joy, all of his love, all of his power, all of his authority, as the Son of God, the Judge of all the earth.

~ 6 ~

BEAUTY WHICH FADETH NOT AWAY

Psalm 90:17

And let the beauty of the LORD our God be upon us: and establish thou the work of our hands upon us; yea, the work of our hands establish thou it. (Psalm 90:17)

Mirrors are wonderful things, but sometimes they are cruel. They detail for us our worst suspicions about the passage of time and the ravages and attacks which the years make upon our appearance. I am told that many people have a jolting, almost physically painful, experience when their mirror shows them the first gray hair, that first sign of baldness, or that line or wrinkle which will not go away even after a good night's sleep. We all have mirrors, and we all use them, but we are slow to see that they are our enemies if we expect always to see in them what we once saw.

I speak of the way we look, for here is a gauge, a thermometer, of what is going on inside of us. The beauty of this life fades away, for we are strangers and pilgrims in the earth. What a cruel trick we play on ourselves when we try to act as if everything will remain the same day after day, year in and year out. All of our puny efforts to beat back time are like trying to stop the inrushing tide of the ocean with a little hill of sand. Maybe we could get along more swiftly with this idea if I could get you to acknowledge here and now, at this moment, that essentially we are helpless creatures, that is, where the big matters are at stake.

We human souls are tempted to believe so many things that are not true but seem like they are true. The Bible with its sound and tested wisdom speaks of this when it says in the book of Proverbs: "There is a way which seemeth right unto a man, but the end thereof are the ways of death" (14:12). Our self-sufficiency seems so beyond the question. When we are young, our teeth seem so

41

unchangeably strong, our step so unalterably firm, our eyesight so permanently clear, our faces so unfailingly smooth and filled with color, that it does not seem possible that these things could ever be different. And our mirrors are, for a while, patient with us. In that strength and physical attractiveness, we seem permanently set. Thus, are we likely to be fooled and misled.

All of this can pass so quickly that we are left dazed as to where the beauty of our faces and the strength of our self-sufficiency went. A young woman reporter has written in a Texas paper of a sudden and serious illness which put her in the hospital for an unforgettable period in her life. She reported that she had always been well groomed: every strand of hair in place, the makeup just right, her body hygiene beyond question, and her nails carefully manicured. And then the hospital: first, there was the indignity of not being on her own. Then her privacy was invaded constantly, and her most intimate bodily functions became semipublic events. The hair could no longer be carefully kept, baths could not be had on whim, and things went sharply downhill. Writing about her experience, this young woman reporter commented on how radically our situations can change and how carefully protected beauty, meaning attractiveness and delightfulness, can be snatched away so quickly.

Along that line, the Bible is not silent. It looks at our human condition in the days of our youthful energy and our early attractiveness. It watches us as we come to the fullness of our vital powers, in the full strength and force of our manhood and womanhood. It smiles at us as we flex our muscles while we carry the loads of life almost casually. The Bible continues to look on us when the first uncertainty as to our permanence and strength brushes up against us ever so slightly. "Nothing to be alarmed about," we think, "just some quirk, a passing reaction — nothing to it." This old Book does not take its eyes off us and sees us with the early energy reduced, the attractive features marred by lines of care, and the eyes darkened by circles of worry. It pronounces its word upon the departure of our physical beauty and strength in the thirty-ninth psalm: "When thou with rebukes dost correct man for iniquity, thou makest his beauty to consume away like a moth: surely every man is vanity" (v. 11).

It is in the light of this that we ought to value all of our notions of what constitutes beauty and attractiveness. Some of us think, especially when we are young, that we can be defiant in life, with a devil-may-care attitude, a toss of the head, and a snapping of the finger. Others think that beauty is totally some external appearance, and we put much store by these most temporary and unreliable accidents of birth. There was a time, for instance, when black people were mesmerized by the majority around them and desperately yearned to look more like white people, while the whites were desperately trying to look more like someone else. Hair was always a problem to black people on these shores — what to do about it and how to get it to look different.

In a fishing camp which I know well, the men, mostly Bostonians, used to trade a lot of good-natured banter and heckling with a man from Charleston, South Carolina, who was a member of one of that city's most prominent black families. The jesting ranged around a certain church where membership was supposedly restricted to black people who could pass the hair test. Now the hair test, so this fishing-camp joking went, was a comb at the entrance of the church. Everyone walked under this comb, with it passing through the hair. If the comb stuck in the hair and did not pass through without trembling, you could not be a member. This man who took it all good-naturedly, one could see, had the kind of hair which would qualify him for membership. Alas, it had almost all gone, and he was nearly bald. "Thou makest his beauty to consume away like a moth" (Psalm 39:11).

Ah, in regard to Christian mothers, and beholding the example of them, I make bold to speak of another kind of beauty which does not depend on any cosmetic device or deception. The psalmist spoke of this beauty in the noble ninetieth, with its grand and measured movements and its sublime thoughts. As the august old song moves to its climactic passage, a prayer breathes forth through the sighs and sobs which have punctuated the psalm, "Let the beauty of the LORD our God be upon us: and establish thou the work of our hands upon us; yea, the work of our hands establish thou it." That word *beauty* is used nearly fifty times in the Scriptures, but only in the book of Psalms do we read of "the beauty of the LORD." We see that term in Psalm 27:4: "One thing have I desired of the LORD, that will I seek after; that I may dwell in the house of the LORD all the days of my life, to behold the beauty of the LORD, and to inquire in his temple." The other time is here in our text, where we see the words "the beauty of the LORD." I know that some translate that word *beauty* as the "goodness" of the Lord, but it seems to be that this prayer is asking that something of what is attractive and delightful in God himself be upon us.

I cannot pretend to be able to define "the beauty of the Lord," and interestingly enough, commentators have not spoken widely of this term, though Matthew Henry refers to the "beauty of the Lord" as his grace and mercy. I believe that I know something of what it means, and I gather my belief from the faces and spirits of some mothers and others on whose brow there seemed to rest nothing less than "the beauty of the Lord," a glow, a brightness, a radiance, and a quiet peacefulness.

Surely, "the beauty of the Lord" has something to do with purpose, for the whole Bible seems to speak of God planning, God intending, and God working toward something he wills to bring to pass in the earth. The Bible starts with purpose: "Let there be," and for God's master creation, humanity, "Let us." All through the Scriptures, that note or purpose runs. Jesus ratified that with the words, "My father worketh hitherto, and I work" (John 5:17). I am tempted to say that "the beauty of the Lord" cannot be on anyone who does not have a purpose and that purpose must be worthy. Drifters know only the awful plunge of Niagara, for the pull or purposelessness is ever downward. Søren Kierkegaard, the earliest of the existentialists, spoke in rebuke of people who are "without any great commitments or goals or purposes." Such, he said, live "always in the moment." Of course, by its very nature a moment quickly passes.

The people I have known who appeared to me to have "the

beauty of the Lord" stamped upon them, and within them, were people of noble and godly purpose. An Irish poet wrote: "He whom a dream hath possessed knoweth no more of doubting." This is not precisely so, but he whom a dream possesses can no longer be captured by doubt. And how in the homes of our community and among our young mothers do we need high and holy purpose for themselves and for their children! Our purpose needs to be to build high standards in our children because Jesus says that we must strive to be perfect as our heavenly Father is perfect. This is a tall order, but then we are tall creatures, made in our spirits of nothing less than the image and likeness of God himself.

Sloppy performance of our daily tasks ill becomes the children of God, and mothers and fathers have the high privilege and the sacred obligation to inculcate in their children a love of excellence. "Whatever is worth doing at all," they taught me when I was young, "is worth doing well." George Bernard Shaw, the celebrated playwright and wit, was a music critic in England and Ireland during the last part of the nineteenth century. He was accused of being severe and of making personal attacks on artists whose performances he reviewed. He said once that some artists he criticized had accused him of personal dislike. Shaw said that they were quite right, adding, "When people do less than their best, and do that less at once badly and complacently, I hate them, loathe them, detest them, long to tear them limb from limb, and strew them about the stage or platform." Herein is a lesson for all of us. To have purpose, a worthy purpose, and to pursue it passionately is a God-given charge. On such a person who, so doing, still trusts God above all else, "the beauty of the Lord" rests.

That leads to one final word. To pursue worthy purpose prayerfully is to bring the "beauty of the Lord," our God, upon us, that beauty which does not fade away. This the world cannot give, and this the world cannot take. Prayer puts beauty on our faces because it puts serenity and peace in our lives. This combination is what William Carey meant and whose thought I paraphrase, "Work as if all depends on you, pray as if all depends on God."

"More things are wrought by prayer / Than this world dreams

of," wrote Alfred, Lord Tennyson. The Scriptures are replete with examples of prevailing prayer. In Genesis 20:17, Abraham prayed unto God until Abimelech, the king of Gerar, was healed. In Numbers 11:2, Moses prayed for a complaining people until the fiery wrath of God was stayed and stopped. In 1 Samuel 1:10, Hannah prayed until God blessed her with the child Samuel. In 2 Kings 6:17, Elisha prayed until a young man's eyes saw horses and chariots of fire in the hills around Dothan. Paul and Silas prayed until a jail in Philippi trembled and the cell doors flew open (Acts 16:25). Jesus prayed in Gethsemane until angels wiped his brow and reinforced his soul (Luke 22:43).

Prayer changes conditions and changes people. A young woman talking on the telephone before singing at a great festival said, "Pray now a little prayer for me," and when the prayer was over, she said, "I feel all right now." A young man wrestling about his vocation was prayed for, and he stood on his feet, saying, "I'm ready now to serve the Lord." Many of us cannot help believing that dear mothers and caring fathers prayed their children away from destruction and toward the Lord Christ.

Here is our highest privilege! We may carry on conversation and communion with God. We are equipped to pray until "heaven comes down our souls to greet and glory crowns the mercy seat." And, yes, to pray on

> Till from Mount Pisgah's lofty height
> I view my home and take my flight:
> This robe of flesh I'll drop, and rise
> To seize the everlasting prize,
> And shout, while passing thru the air,
> "Farewell, farewell, sweet hour of prayer!"

∾ 7 ∾

BEING GLAD ABOUT BEING A CHRISTIAN

Mark 2:18–19

And the disciples of John and of the Pharisees used to fast: and they come and say unto him, Why do the disciples of John and of the Pharisees fast, but thy disciples fast not? And Jesus said unto them, Can the children of the bridechamber fast, while the bridegroom is with them? as long as they have the bridegroom with them, they cannot fast. (Mark 2:18–19)

"Thy disciples fast not," they said to Jesus. It was half question, half rebuke. Ever, people have associated a frown with religion. There is a certain suspicion on the part of many people if one who claims to be a Christian seems too lighthearted and merry. We feel more sure about the authenticity and reality of people's Christian faith if they do not smile too easily, if they seem to be having an unpleasant time from day to day. Gladness in a Christian is for many people a sign of something lacking in the quality of discipleship.

Granted, there are many forms of gladness that ought to be deeply suspect and about which we ought to raise the most serious doubts and questions. There is the gladness of idiots who do not know what is going on around them. One shudders in the presence of the vacant stare and the soulless laughter of someone whose mental equipment has gone askew and is out of order. It is sad, indeed, to see gladness and hear laughter from someone who is oblivious to what is happening. You remember the lines from that well-known poem: "If you can keep your head when all about you / Are losing theirs and blaming it on you, ... you'll be a Man, my son!" A friend I know has paraphrased that to say, "If you can keep your head when all about you are losing theirs and blaming it on you, then you don't know what's going on."

47

Away with the gladness of idiots who see no evil, hear no evil, and speak no evil because they do not know what is happening.

There is likewise the gladness of those who know exactly what is happening but figure the terrible consequences will occur only in the distant future. Fearful things are in the offing; the day of reckoning will surely come, but later. You remember Scarlett O'Hara in *Gone with the Wind* saying again and again about impending trouble, "I'll think about that tomorrow." One of the famous historical illustrations of such unhealthy gladness is to be found in the well-known comment of Jeanne Antoinette, marquise de Pompadour, mistress of Louis XV of France. Basking in the most lavish luxury in her tastefully decorated home at Bellevue in the Paris suburb of Saint Cloud while France tottered on the edge of ruin and its armies collapsed before the savage onslaught of the soldiers of Frederick the Great in the battle of Rossbach, Madame Pompadour said to Louis, "After us the deluge." Many a fool is glad in the illusion that payday for folly will come someday, but after he or she is gone. To use one other and more recent example, a figure of shame is the English prime minister with the umbrella, Neville Chamberlain, leaving Munich in 1938 believing he had appeased the nationalist lust and insanity of Adolf Hitler and announcing to the world that he had secured peace in "our time," only to see the blitzkrieg of the German military machine swallow Poland and threaten all of Europe.

The gladness of the Christian is neither the mindless grin of the idiot nor the smug smile of those who think that they will never have to face the consequences of their folly and wickedness. The gladness of a Christian is structured and situated around Jesus Christ. Have you not heard someone bearing a tense and expectant congregation before the throne of mercy express a supreme gladness and thankfulness for Jesus Christ? "We thank you, Father, for food and shelter, for family and friends, for our neighbors and our neighbor's children, but above all, we thank you for Jesus."

It is what the Lord has done in your life that ought to make you glad, full of joy and good feeling through and through. In fact, a true believer in Jesus has no business living any length of time in low and melancholy valleys of depression. To be sure, we all must camp near the swamps of sadness and sorrow and defeat now and again, but Christians ought not to live there.

Jesus said that wherever he is, gladness and joy are the mood of those around him. There were those who watched his disciples while he was here on earth. The regnant mood, the key characteristic, of early Christian people was a kind of celebration, a gladness, as if life had turned into one perpetual banquet and one unending party.

Those who thought they knew what religion was all about did not like the way the disciples of Jesus conducted themselves. They were glad people who found it, as one preacher put it, difficult to think of anything but the amazing thing that had befallen them. Jesus Christ had made their lives a banquet, a party, a joy, a celebration.

So some who were puzzled, and maybe a little vexed, by this gaiety and joy on the part of the friends of Jesus got up enough courage and came to Jesus to put the question bluntly to him whether it was proper for sincerely religious, godly people to be so full of laughter and gladness as were the disciples of Jesus. The Master came back with the reply that is the text: "Can the wedding guests fast while the bridegroom is with them?" It was to say that where Jesus is, it is joy like a wedding, gladness like a celebration. The party's on; in Jesus, regal good times roll. You're talking about a ball, a big time, but the worlding does not begin to know what a good time is. People who love the Lord, people to whom Jesus is precious, people who move in the soft sunshine and gentle winds of the Lord's presence, are having a happy time, a celebration, all of the time. Anywhere and everywhere is party time for God's people. We can laugh, sing, shout, pray, clap hands. "Jesus is mine and I am his forevermore, and the world can't do me no harm," so my forebears sang.

Christians are glad when they look back, for everything has been cleared. Old differences between us and God have been straightened out. There was an old charge against us, but, thank God, in

Jesus the charge has been dropped, our record has been cleared, and we have been restored to full citizenship and given the gainful employment of thanking and praising the Lord and rejoicing in the God of our salvation. It is all right when we look back; the old account is settled, and the record is clear today. That truth stands in our history. Every enemy of freedom, every plan of disparity and injustice, no matter how elaborately conceived and implemented, has failed in this country, often in spite of wealth and influence.

Yes, when we look back, we can be glad in Jesus because he has brought us all this journey through. When we remember the road behind us, we remember that the Lord has held our hand and guided our footsteps. He has beaten back the dark clouds and smoothed out our pathway. He has brought us a mighty long way, through briers and thickets, and has led us sometimes in shady green pastures so rich and so sweet. God has led us. "Sometimes where the water's cool flow bathes the weary one's feet, God has led us along. Sometimes on the mount where the sun shines so bright, sometimes in the valley in the darkest of night, God has led his dear children along." The old hymn is right: "Through many dangers, toils, and snares, we have already come." We can be truly glad when we look back.

We can be glad when we look around, for the way is growing brighter every passing day. I, for one, am enjoying the presence and the power of the Lord right now. Christians can be glad when they look around, for it is well with their souls. There are those who accuse us of being a "pie-in-the-sky-by-and-by" people. Yes, we've got that, but now we are marching through Immanuel's ground. Right now, God's people are feasting on manna from a bountiful supply. Right now, we are drinking from a fountain that never shall run dry. As Kitty Parham sings, "The Lord is blessing me right now." When I look around, I am glad that I am his and he is forever mine, that "he walks with me, and he talks with me, And he tells me I am his own." If there were no tomorrow, I would thank God that he and I are friends now, that beneath the shadow of his wings my defenseless soul can hide while the storm is passing over.

Great national difficulties arise. The nation seems to have lost its confidence about the Republic's destiny, but God is at work even now, and yonder voices are lifted calling the nation to keep faith with its noblest impulses and highest purposes. They will prevail because God is in history to make his story.

When we look ahead, we who are God's people can be glad, for we are the possessors of a rich and precious promise. He has promised that he will get us all the way: "He shall deliver thee in six troubles: yea in seven there shall be no evil touch thee." We cannot know what the coming days may bring; harder yet may be the fight. And, as the hymn has it, right may often yield to might, but we can be sure that God is able to get us all of the way.

We may fall sometimes, but he will pick us up. We cannot know whether sickness or sorrow will be our fate, but the Lord has promised that he will guide until the day is done. Somewhere and somehow in God's own time, the shadows must flee away. Somewhere and somehow in God's own time, the load must lift, and the clouds must rift. Somewhere and somehow in God's own time, we are going to reach the top of the mountain. Somewhere and somehow there is a bright side; don't you rest until you find it. Somewhere and somehow in God's own time, we are to see the King in the beauty of his holiness and the holiness of his beauty. Somewhere and somehow in God's own time, his will *will* be done on earth as it is in heaven. And so, we march on into our tomorrows. We have only to keep faith with the bright visions the Lord has given us, and we may be sure that we shall come "to an older place than Eden / And a taller town than Rome." God has willed it so!

∾ 8 ∾

BELIEVING AND SEEING

John 11:40

Jesus saith unto her, Said I not unto thee, that, if thou wouldest believe, thou shouldest see the glory of God? (John 11:40)

I think if we will look squarely at ourselves, at our spirit, we will discover, we will be aware, that the Lord Jesus both attracts and repels us. There is something so attractive about the name, about the person, about the spirit, and about the words of our Lord that many of us feel irresistibly drawn to him. But there is also some quality, something earnest — I had started to say severe, but that is not the right word — something almost terrifyingly earnest about him that makes us draw back. If you will look at your own Christian life carefully enough, you will discover that it is made up of that combination of attraction and repulsion, of being drawn toward and falling back from. His words, the things he says to us, his whole way seems to cut against the grain of what we are all about. It is against the tide of our makeup, and it takes nothing short of grace to get us, in — what is that word they use now? — in "sync," in line with him because he cuts across our grain. For instance, when he says to us, "Did somebody make you go a mile?" Well our natural grain is — if we have to do it — to go frowning and pouting. That is our natural grain; that's the way the grain runs. But he says that if somebody makes you go a mile, when you reach the end of that mile, you volunteer for the second one.

Now my late friend, whose funeral I preached in Chicago years ago, J. C. Austin used to say, "You've got a chance on the second mile to do something constructive because you are doing a favor the second mile; you've been forced the first one." But it cuts against our grain. Then when he says to us that if somebody slaps you on one cheek — and he does not mean turn the other because you've swung a roundhouse and you've been pulled around — turn the other cheek. It goes against the grain. It takes a lot of grace for us to even begin to deal with what Jesus tells us and what he shows us. There is another place where he cuts against the grain. We, with our shrewdness and our slickness and knowing our way around, as we say — we assert, "Seeing is believing." Or, "What you see is what you get." "I am from Missouri; show me." "I'll believe it when I see it." These are natural. He cuts across that grain and says here in this passage, "If thou would believe, thou should see the glory of God." We say, seeing is believing; he says, believing is seeing.

The circumstance, of course, grows out of the death of Lazarus. Jesus informs his disciples when Lazarus has died that "our friend Lazarus is asleep." One wonders why he would say that he was asleep. Maybe, maybe our Lord had forgotten the people he was talking to. He started talking the language of his native land. That word *death* does not occur in the dictionary of eternity. It's an earth word. They've got no word in the better country for death, and there is a reason why. Our words grow out of our experiences. Words do not — some people have argued this more recently — do not create things, but things create words.

In the country which was native to our Lord, his own land, there is no word for death. But they've got no word because they've got no death. And it may be, on the other hand, he may have been breaking the news gradually to them: "Lazarus is asleep." But they said to him, "Well if Lazarus is asleep, that's good." Then he said to them, "Lazarus is dead."

Then they start off for the house at Bethany where Mary and Martha and their brother Lazarus lived. This is their only brother as far as we know, and the sisters are heartbroken. When Jesus gets there — Lazarus is dead. There's not any more one can say on that, in human terms. This is finality. We try to rescue something out of that by asking, "What was his trouble? What did he die with?" Well that really does not make much difference. That's just a little way that we try to ease the thing to some degree. If he is dead, it makes very little difference with what he died. That is our little accommodation; we don't know anything else to say. There isn't much else to say, talking humanly. If one doesn't have some kind of religious spirit, that is all one can say.

Dead, Lazarus is dead. Our Lord is talking here about finality. Kaput! Finis! The end! No more! It's over! Lazarus is dead! He says, "Take me where you've buried him." They said to him, "Look, it has been four days now. His body, he's. . . . " Well they put it bluntly and said, "He's has been dead four days." Putrefaction has set in; decomposition has begun. Not only is Lazarus dead, but the body is decomposed. Finality! Finality!

There's something about the way of our Christ that does not try to seek only that which is easy. In the instance of Lazarus, we are face to face with what to the most superb human power is hopelessness — utter, total helplessness. Martha expresses for all of us a sense of finality beyond which it is futile to hold out hope. Standing at the grave, Jesus makes a request — or was it a command? "Take away the stone." Martha replies that there is no use. Her brother has been dead four days. Decomposition will have set in. There can only be a stench coming from the opened sepulcher. Yet the imperious word of Jesus is "Carry me to the tomb."

Standing at the grave, "Jesus wept." This leaves us utterly defenseless. Here Jesus shows us a quality of God that brings us to our knees. Once, years ago at Texas Christian University, I heard a New Testament scholar say that the principle teaching of the New Testament is that of a God whose ways are like Jesus'. Believing that, as I do, when we come to the grave of Lazarus and see Jesus weep, we are brought inevitably to the conclusion that God can suffer. This is the passibility of the Eternal. It is enough to snatch the breath away.

That we see God reflected in Jesus may well be the reason Paul's great trinitarian benediction at the end of 2 Corinthians begins, not with God, but with Christ. Paul says, "The grace of the Lord Jesus Christ, and the love of God, and the communion of the Holy Ghost be with you all." So! We come to behold the "love of God" by way of "the grace of the Lord Jesus Christ."

An English poet has pictured what may be cause for greater sorrow in God's heart. He pictured Christ appearing at Charing Cross in London at the hour of the hurrying throng's busiest time. There stood Christ with the nail prints and the crown of thorns, reaching out for friendship. The crowd, too busy with their own affairs, passed by, never seeing him. And Christ sadly longed for Calvary — that would be more merciful. "Jesus wept."

One of the meanings of the Creation is that God wanted someone with whom he would have communion, conversation, and fellowship. Mighty animals whose footfalls almost made the forest tremble were not eligible. So God made us — with the high honor of choice. So often, we decide against the God who made us. Still this power of choice was the only way God could have a creature able to think his thoughts after him. Our refusal of God's company is cause for the tears of God.

The power of Christ is not finally frustrated by his tears. He summons Lazarus from the grave. The crux of the account is that *God* is final. Beyond the limitations of our humanity, there is access to capability. The lesson for us is that we must never believe that there are circumstances and conditions that lie beyond the authority and ability of the eternal God. So believing and so trusting and so venturing forth into our future, whatever it might be, we shall find ourselves conquerors and "more than conquerors, through him that loved us."

∽ 9 ∾

BRIGHT SONGS IN DARK NIGHTS

Job 35:10

But none saith, Where is God my maker, who giveth songs in the night? (Job 35:10)

I speak this morning on the subject "Bright Songs in Dark Nights." The text is from the tenth verse of the thirty-fifth chapter of the book of Job: "But none saith, Where is God my maker, who giveth songs in the night?" This is a wonderful old book; it walks around our human condition and weeps with us when we are sad and offers us something for our weeping. It points a finger at us when we are wrong and tells how to get right. It rejoices with us in the days of our success and tells us not to forget the source from which good gifts come. It is a wonderful old book. And I pray to God that, as the fall comes and our Bible readers start again, more of us will seek to find the strength that is in it. It criticizes us in our individual personalities; it reminds our society and our government when they are wrong.

I spent some days working with preachers in the East Ohio Methodist Conference on preaching the other week. Their question was, "How can you preach about things that people do not like to hear, particularly in their tribal guilt, of government and what not?" And I said to them, "As long as you come at them out of Scripture, they have no right to get angry at you, but let them get angry with the Author, whose messenger you merely are." This Bible is divided into what we call the Old Testament and the New Testament. The Old Testament takes a particular people, Israel, and out of that particularity universalizes so that all people

---

This sermon was preached in the wake of a fearsome denominational struggle when the work of Martin Luther King Jr. was in jeopardy. This rendering reveals the impossibility of recording the spoken word in print. — *GCT*

see themselves from one people. It is what I think the logicians, and what not, call "deductive reasoning." It is reasoning from a general principle to a specific one.

So we see ourselves reflected there in the Old Testament. If I were to ask you this morning, "What is the most influential book in the Old Testament?" I think I know the answer! I think that everyone would say, "The book of Psalms." I would grant you that it touches us more widely, at more points of our human need, at more of our varying, vagrant, sifting moods, than any other book. It speaks about when we are angry and when we are glad, when we feel vindictive and vengeful toward others, and when we are worshipful. It is old Israel's hymnbook. But if I were to ask, "What is that book that deals more profoundly and completely with the great supreme question of human life?" I think the answer would have to be, "The book of Job."

There is hardly any question that is so recurring and in certain times so pressing as the question, "Why?" It has haunted our human journey. We hear it from our Lord in the extremities of his suffering upon Calvary: "My God, my God, why?" When something comes upon us, that is the question which rushes to the front: "Why?" You have said it, and you have heard it: "Why me? Why me?" No book deals so persistently, so stubbornly, with the matter of that great question of human suffering, and how God relates to our human suffering as does the book of Job. It is set in the form of a drama. And it ought to be read as such. There are characters that come in one by one and sit around a man on a bed, a pallet to be more exact, of festering sores as he contemplates the ruin of his fortune, the death of his children, and the disease which riddles his body.

I cannot think of a more memorable night in a Broadway theater than that night I sat and watched the unfolding of Archibald MacLeish's drama *J. B.*, on Job. And I can still see the actor who played Job, with the lights beating upon him on the floor of the stage, with that awful look in his eyes and his hands raised imploringly to the heavens, "Why?" That is the great question of human life. Of course it ought to be asked, on both sides, of our human experience, not alone when we are grief stricken. But we also ought to ask it when things go well with us. Why? If we do not deserve the bad, which I will be talking about in a minute since that occupies more of our consideration than the other, if we do not deserve the bad, we most assuredly do not deserve the good.

There are these characters. They make an appointment to see Job. They communicated some way with each other and decided that they would meet as Job's house. He was their friend; they had undoubtedly enjoyed many an evening together, and now Job was sick. They sat on the floor and started off on the wrong track. They sat there around his pallet of sickness and stared at him for seven days, which leads me to say that we ought really learn how to see the sick. People in pain do not need to have someone staring at them. That look we can get on our faces when we see somebody in the extremities of illness which says, "How in the name of God did you get like that?" is the wrong way to see sick people.

One of them said that nobody suffers unless they've done wrong, which is a lie. Jesus suffered. Saints suffer and sinners suffer, too, but with a difference. Still saints suffer. One of Job's comforters said, "You suffer because you have done wrong." If Job *had* done wrong, that was not the time to say it. When Job tried to answer, another said, "You're not doing a thing but using words; your words are full of wind." Another said to him, "What you're doing in claiming innocence is trying to avoid criticism because you're sick. And you're sick because you've done wrong." Note that was what his friends said. Now, I submit to you that with three friends like that, you would hardly need any enemies. How sad!

I have a childhood memory. I had a tendon pulled in my neck, and some of the fellows came to see me. I was a lad and they started telling me how wonderful it was pitching horseshoes up in the next block. That's not the way to see the sick. You ought not go in to see the sick telling them how wonderful the weather is outside, what a wonderful time you had yesterday or last night.

That's not the way to see the sick. When we ask whether or not the pastor has been to see the sick one, it makes a comparison. "See, I am here. Has so-and-so come to see you?" This is often by way of complimenting ourselves and criticizing others.

In a hospital that I knew, forty-odd years ago, the administrators stopped some religious people from having special visiting rights. The doctors were trying to heal people, and here were these religious people coming in and singing, "Am I born to die, and to lay my body down?" That is the wrong way. We need to develop some sensitivity.

How often in the Bible night is referred to as the time for rest. But more so, night is looked upon as a time of terror and danger; there are nights of sorrow and the night of sickness. As someone said, "We long for the morning more than they that are sick." In the sickroom, night is often a dreadful time. When everything is still and the body is aching, one looks for the morning that one thinks will never come.

Now nobody welcomes such a nighttime, and we ought to remember that the sky is a parable for our lives in a way. Day comes and then night comes. We cannot avoid this rhythm. Nobody welcomes the nights of testing, those times when things go awry. When life is not its most pleasant, when we are being tested by sickness or by disappointment, when friends seem to be putting the knife in our back — nobody welcomes this.

Indeed, there is something wrong with anybody who is eager for this. Anyone who does is not "playing with all the clubs in the bag." There are some people who have a form of illness and who really court the darkness. They are most at home when things are bad. They seem to get their enjoyment out of complaining. Their pleasure is in finding what is wrong. They are uncomfortable when things are going along well. And some of them, if things are going along well, will start trouble because they feel more at home when there is confusion and trouble. They love confusion; they are seekers after conflict.

Did I ever tell you about a deacon I knew in another place? I think the reason I have gotten along so well with you men, and those who sat in those places before you, is due not only to your good spirit but to contrasting you with that deacon I knew in the long ago. He was a good man — God knows he was, almost painfully good — but I never saw him smile. I saw once or twice a little twitch in the jaw, but it never really worked out to a smile. He was serious all of the time and he meant no harm. He was a friend to me, a young pastor then. I remember his saying to me, "Brother Taylor, we're not being 'buked enough for the Lord." (This was our black word for 'rebuke' once.) Well, dealing with him, I thought *I* was being 'buked enough for the Lord. That man was in love with suffering and that is not healthy. If you enjoy things not being right, the elevator is not going quite to the top floor. Yet, these things must come. This is what the book of Job is all about. These things must come. Sometimes when our children are growing up, we wish we could spare them some things, but these things must come. You and I will never grow up into what God wants us to be unless sometime it is nighttime.

Aquila Matthews lived in Atlantic City and was one of the leading citizens of that city. She was greatly gifted in music. She told once of a young woman with a marvelous voice for singing. A man who had been soundly trained in music heard her sing and said to her, "You are going to be a great singer one day." She, in her youth eager to get the brass ring, you know, to reach the goal said, "When?" He said, "As soon as your heart gets broken." Tough business, but that's what it's all about. You and I will never grow up to what God wants us to be until we learn to pass through the nighttime. When things go against us, when we are put to the test, when every nerve is on edge, when we are under stress, when we do not know how it is going to turn out, when it looks like it will not turn out right — you and I need that.

Frances Perkins was secretary of labor during the administration of Franklin Roosevelt. She said that she saw Mr. Roosevelt in his earliest years, scion of a family of privilege in Hyde Park, graduate of Harvard. When later she saw him after paralysis had twisted his body, she said she saw a different man. At first there was, she thought, a certain easy, not malicious, arrogance about him, but when his body had been racked by pain, a new light came in his eyes, a new tenderness in his heart. The only way we're going to become the acceptable people of God is by enduring nighttime. When things seem against us, when our spirits are cast down, when the world seems not on our side, that experience does something for us, does something to our spirit.

There is a lesson to be learned in the house of sorrow that the house of laughter can never teach. For one we learn fellow feeling. We learn how to sympathize with other people, how to feel other people's hurts. We learn how to understand what causes them to cry when we learn to cry ourselves. We need that in order to be truly human. If you want to be some kind of fake walking around, then avoid everything that puts you under stress. Escape out of every situation that is unpleasant. Do you want to be a fake? Is that your goal in life to be a counterfeit article? Then laugh all of the time. Don't let anything touch you, don't let it get inside of you, don't let anything hurt you — if you want to be a fake. But if you want to be real, and if you want to be what God wants you to be, you have to learn to accept these experiences of the night, those times when the soul passes through darkness and trial.

I hear Jesus as he faces his cross saying, "The cup which my Father gives me, ought not I drink of it?" That gives us a fellow feeling with the Savior as almost nothing else does. In turn, we learn to feel more keenly what other people are facing when we face something ourselves. Our nighttime of difficulty can increase our faith in God, can teach us how to pray. Now, I am not talking about using some sentences; I am talking about praying. I am talking about talking to God as if, almost as if, he's a natural man. I'm talking about pleading with him and staying there and hanging and knocking on the door and refusing to let go and refusing to leave, begging, arguing.

You'll never learn that in the daytime when things go well with you, but you will learn it when you are up against something that's too big for you. You don't know how to handle it, and it looks like you don't have a friend in the world and nobody to help you anywhere, and you've got nowhere to turn, except to the Lord. You'll learn then how to call his name and ask him, for God gives us, if we will turn to him, bright songs in dark nights. We learn then that no matter how dark the night is, there must be some reason. I read in the Bible that Christ, "though he were a son, yet learned he obedience by the things which he suffered." That's in the fifth chapter in the book of Hebrews at the eighth verse. And do I not read somewhere else that "whom the Lord loveth, he chasteneth"? Despise not the chastisements of the Lord, for he makes the wounds, and he maketh whole. And we learn in the dark nights, when everything seems to be going against us, when we're swimming against the tides and the burden presses down heavy upon us and our pillows are damp with our tears — we learn that in a world where God lives, if night comes, morning is sure to come. "Weeping may endure for the night, but joy cometh in the morning," in a world where God lives. My late cousin, professional soldier Leonard Harris, put it another way: "If it is good, enjoy it. If is bad, endure it. Neither will last."

I wish to God that you would go with me in imagination to the old Roman garrison city of Philippi. Two men are strangers in that town, Paul and Silas. They have been arrested, and they have been beaten, as was the preliminary penalty in many cases of what we call "Roman justice." They were thrown in jail in Philippi. They had no influential friends in that city. There was no one who might have made the difference in that town, on whom they might have called. They had done no wrong except that they had told about Jesus and what he had done for them and what he would do for others. For that they were thrown into this dark and, of course, unlighted dungeon. The sun went down on them that evening; the shades of darkness gathered around that cell. It was night. That night, because they knew the Lord, they knew that he could, if he chose, do whatever it was they wanted but would surely do what was best for them. I want you to carry that home. The Lord could do if he chose what they wanted but would surely do what was best for them. So that night that Philippian jail heard a strange sound. The city lay locked in silence and sleep.

I imagine, as Clarence Macartney did before me, that that Philippian jail with its old stone dungeon had heard many sounds — the groans of the bruised, the angry shrieks of those who felt they were wrongly jailed, the piteous cries of people who felt desperate, many sounds — but it never had heard what it heard that night. Do you know what? The account says that at the darkest time of night, in the middle of the night when light was farthest away and darkness was closest and most daunting, at the time when lonesomeness was at its worst, that jail heard something that it had never heard before. The Scripture says that at midnight with no sign of morning anywhere, at midnight with no life to cheer their weariness, at midnight when no visitors could come in to see how they were, at midnight, Paul and Silas prayed, talked to God, and then sang, sang at midnight, sang in the jail, sang with the handcuffs on them, sang with the leg irons around their ankles, sang, sang praises unto God, sang in the jail, sang bound in prison, sang with no friends anywhere, sang.

I don't know what they sang. I imagine that they must have picked up that Twenty-third Psalm: "Yea, though I walk through the valley of the shadow of death, I will fear no evil: for thou art with me." Maybe Silas raised that hymn, the twenty-seventh: "The Lord is my light and my salvation...of whom shall I be afraid?" And maybe they sang from Isaiah, "When thou passest through the waters, I will be with thee; and through the rivers, they shall not overflow thee: when thou walkest through the fire, thou shalt not be burned....For I am the LORD thy God." They sang. They sang until the soreness got out of their bodies; they sang until the handcuffs turned their spirits loose; they sang until the leg irons could not hold their climbing aspirations; they sang until the earth shook; they sang until the prison trembled; they sang until the cell door fell open; they sang until the power of the Lord came down. They sang. They sang until "heaven came down their souls to greet and glory crowned the mercy seat." They sang. God can give you bright songs, I know what I speak of, can give you bright songs in dark nights.

~ 10 ~

WIDE VISIONS FROM A NARROW WINDOW

Job 19:25–27

For I know that my redeemer liveth, and that he shall stand at
the latter day upon the earth: And though after my skin worms
destroy this body, yet in my flesh shall I see God: Whom I shall see
for myself, and mine eyes shall behold. (Job 19:25–27)

I want to try to deal tonight with a "wide vision from a narrow
window." In the nineteenth chapter of the book of Job, there are
these well-known words: "For I know that my redeemer liveth,
and that he shall stand at the latter day upon the earth: And
though after my skin worms destroy this body, yet in my flesh
shall I see God: Whom I shall see for myself, and mine eyes shall
behold." These words have lighted the darkness for twenty-five
centuries of human living. They touch us in a peculiar way. In my
own congregation as our dead are led out into the light for the
last time, they are repeated: "I know that my redeemer liveth."

Wherever men and women have thought seriously about the issues of life, they have pondered these words and the sentiments of
the book of Job, this ancient drama of suffering and of a suffering
shot through by a presence, of suffering examined and suffering
redeemed. Once, years ago on Broadway, I along with great numbers of people, fashionable people in my city, sat one evening and
watched the reenactment of this ancient drama — Archibald Mac-
Leish's *J. B.* — in modern dress. Why has this ancient account
lived on to be considered and examined and reflected upon by the
succeeding generations of twenty-five centuries? "Why?" you ask
me. And I answer, "Because these words of this book speak of
the deepest and truest stuff of our human existence." This whole
book of Job is an accurate transcript of what human life is all
about. It is a biopsy, a sample of living tissue, of what our human
condition is all about. It speaks of tears and laughter, of joy and

sorrow, of health and sickness, of prosperity and adversity, of sunshine and storms, of fair weather and foul, all touched by the living presence of the everlasting God. And, my brothers, and particularly young men who preach, these are items that never go out of style, for men weep and laugh in all cultures and in all languages. They hope and despair in all cultures, and there is a brooding presence over all of human life wherever it is lived, for all of our lives are lived under the gaze of God: *sub specie aeternitatis,* under the very light of eternity. That's why the book lives on.

The nineteenth chapter finds a man confronting his friends who have for eighteen chapters confronted him. They have accused and indicted and condemned and blamed him for eighteen chapters. He can bear it no longer, and the nineteenth chapter is his reply to their gloomy countenances and their long, bitter indictment of his calamity as they sit around the pallet of his misery. He says to them at last, "Why will you vex my soul?" The window has narrowed out of which he looks upon the landscape of life. Once, there had been the homes of children and fruitful fields and grazing cattle and bleating sheep. But now the window has narrowed. He lies amidst the graves of his children and the ruin of his fortune. But then, beyond that, his own body is attacked, as is the legacy of our human plight and condition. And his friends have assaulted him. They have driven cold steel into his already bleeding spirit. They have added indignity upon indignity, and they have visited insult upon insult, and he can bear it no longer. The window out of which he looks at the landscape of life has narrowed to a slit. But beyond what they have said to him, he says to them, "Why will you vex my soul and break me in pieces with words? Ten times have you reproached me. You are not ashamed that you make yourselves strange to me and maybe I have erred, I said but why will you magnify it?" The window narrows out of which he looks upon the landscape of his existence.

But beyond that, he says that God seems to be his enemy. We humans can bear almost anything if in the darkness of our human plight, when we reach out, our hands trembling and pleading, if the great hands that "once weighed the mountains in scales and the hills in balances" (Isaiah 40:12) will take hold of our hand. We can bear almost anything. Here the window narrows out of which Job looks upon the landscape of his existence. In addition to his friends, so called, who sit around and catalog the reasons found in the failures of his own soul as to his plight, he says, "It seems that God has overthrown me." Here is where the window narrows to a slit. If God be for us, then what difference does it make who is against us? If God be for us, then our enemies are like dust. If God be with us, then calamity can come only so close. If God be with us, we can "run through a troop and jump over a wall." But if God be against us, what else is there left?

I do not know why in the solemn appointments of God that there are times that it does indeed seem as if we've got not a friend on earth or in heaven left. I know that God saves us, and P. T. Forsyth said this in his Lyman Beecher Lectures of 1907, not by flattering us but by opposing us. Preacher, you say that you want great power to move among people's heartstrings. You cannot have that without great sorrow. God can fill only the place that has been emptied of the joys of this life. Do your research. R. W. Dole, at Carrs Lane Church, laying in Birmingham, England, had particularly toward the end a terribly lonely existence. Charles Spurgeon in the Metropolitan Tabernacle had rheumatism and gout that made life unbearable for him. Frederick W. Robertson at Brighton was so sensitive that the least thing shattered him like the piercing of an eye. George Truett, who charmed the American South in the first four decades of this century, lived in the after-memory of a hunting accident in which a friend was killed by Truett's own gun. This institute is named for L. K. Williams. A friend, not a preacher, said that he visited the Williams's home with Dr. Williams's son, who was then a student at Morehouse, and he said that Dr. Williams sat in the twilight, and his voice seemed so sad. It was some inward tide of sorrow. Is it not said even of our Lord that he "became obedient unto the cross"?

Such a great word is written there in the ravishing visions of the Revelation when search is made for somebody who is able to open the seals and to read the inscrutable mysteries of our human destiny. John said that an angel searched through the heavens and found among the heavenly creatures nobody worthy to open the book, not even those pure beings who endlessly cry, "Holy, holy, holy," around the lily-white throne. No one was found from the tier upon tier of the angelic chorus who sing their perfect anthems everlastingly to the glory of the one who sits upon the throne. Not in earth nor beneath the earth. But when one did come forth and take the book and break the seals, there rang through the heavens resounding anthems of praise and thanksgiving: "Thou art worthy for thou wast slain." The blood marks in the hand are the seal of authority. Now you may tickle people's fancy, but you will never preach to their hearts until at some place some solemn appointment has fallen upon your own life and you have wept bitter tears and gone through your own Gethsemane and climbed your own Calvary. That's where power is! It is not in the tone of the voice; it is not in the eloquence of the preacher; it is not in the gracefulness of his gestures; it is not in the magnificence of his congregation; it is in a heart broken and put together again by the eternal God.

"God has overthrown me and has trapped me in his net" (Job 19:6). The window narrows.

> He hath fenced up my way that I cannot pass, and he hath set darkness in my paths. God hath stripped me, stripped me of my glory. God has taken the crown from off my head. God hath destroyed me on every side. God. And my hope hath he removed like a tree. God hath kindled his wrath against me. And he hath counted me unto him as one of his enemies. His troops come together and raise up their way against me and encamp around about my tabernacle. He hath put my brethren far from me, and my acquaintances are estranged from me. My kinfolk have failed, and my familiar friends have forgotten me. They that dwell in my house count me for a stranger; I am an alien in their sight. I called my servant, and he gave me no answer. My breath is strange to my wife. Young children despise me; I arose and they spake against me. All my inward friends have abhorred me. My bones cleaveth to my skin and to my flesh. (vv. 8–20, *paraphrased*)

How will Job answer? That is the pivotal question of life. Some people cry out against God when calamity falls heavily upon them. Thomas Hardy spoke of it... "that dumb dark thing that turns the handle of this idle show," speaking of God. How will this man answer? How do you answer when the tide goes against you, when it seems like you have no hiding place and your head is defenseless underneath the unfriendly elements? How do you answer in the deep, dark places of the soul where the sides of the valley rise steep around you and there is no sunlight on your pathway? How do you answer when it seems that all light is gone and all that you once counted dear is against you? How do you answer? The window has narrowed to a slit.

This man takes the pus-filled sores and separates them as the scabs come off from the pallet, gets up to look out. Out there he sees a broad landscape. "I know that my redeemer lives." He is saying that there is a God somewhere. When we look out upon our nation, having avoided the confrontations of God so often in our existence and now moving however sadly toward some unknown valley, we know that there is a God somewhere. When one sees those who rose to power on thinly shielded bigotry, we will still assert that there is a God somewhere. When standard bearers of the darkest bigotry in the South have lost their hold even upon their religion, we must conclude that there is, indeed, a God somewhere. The night may grow very dark, but there is a God somewhere.

And then Job goes on to say, and gives that great foreshadowing which belongs to all great faith, that the best is yet to be. You see, secular societies place their golden age in the past. It takes high religion to see the best ahead. That's the great eschatological hope of the Christian life. If I read the theme of the biblical revelation aright, that theme of bright future runs all through Scripture: the great "shall" and "will be" of God. One sees it again and again: "The scepter *shall* not depart from Judah, nor a lawgiver from between his feet, until Shiloh come; and unto him *shall* the gathering of the people be." "The lion and the lamb *shall* lie down together." "They *shall* not hurt nor destroy in all my holy hill." "Every valley *shall* be exalted; every mountain *shall* be brought low; the crooked way *shall* be made straight; the crooked places *shall* be made plain. The glory of the LORD *shall* be revealed, and all flesh *shall* see it together." "They that wait upon the LORD *shall* renew their strength; they *shall* mount up with wings of eagles. They *shall* run and not be weary; they *shall* walk and not faint." And when I come to the New Testament that "shall" stands: "You *shall* see the Son of man coming in power." And as the Revelation closes, "there *shall* be no more curse, and they *shall* see his face, and his name *shall* be in their forehead, and they *shall* worship him, and they *shall* reign with him forever and ever." Yes, the night may be dark, but the morning is sure to come. The way may be hard, but it is bound to smooth out.

﹏ 11 ﹏

CHARIOTS AFLAME

Joshua 17:18; 2 Kings 6:17

> But the mountain shall be thine; for it is a wood, and thou shalt cut
> it down: and the outgoings of it shall be thine: for thou shalt drive
> out the Canaanites, though they have iron chariots, and though
> they be strong. (Joshua 17:18)

> And Elisha prayed, and said, LORD, I pray thee, open his eyes, that
> he may see. And the LORD opened the eyes of the young man; and
> he saw: and, behold, the mountain was full of horses and chariots
> of fire round about Elisha. (2 Kings 6:17)

We live in a world of sense and things and must come to terms
with them. "A man has to eat," someone says, and sensible people
agree, except that choice human spirits such as Gandhi have re-
fused to eat in service of high purpose. I am against a disembodied
faith which does not take into account that we have to live amidst
physical sights and sound. A ghost Christianity cut loose from the
earth — misty, vaporous, suspended, so to speak, in midair — does
not honor our Lord Jesus. If the coming of Jesus Christ among us
means anything, it means that God respected, honored, chose, this
theater of food and clothing, shelter, things, money, touchables,
as a setting worthy of the presence of the Son of God. Our Lord
Jesus Christ put physical, down-to-earth considerations right in
the middle of the prayer he gave us as our model of petition to
the Father. Did not our Lord tell us to ask God for daily physical
food? "Give us this day our daily bread" (Matthew 6:11).

Joshua spoke to Ephraim and Manasseh of actual physical
reality, touchable, substantial material things: "But the mountain
shall be thine; for it is a wood, and thou shalt cut it down: and the
outgoings of it shall be thine: for thou shalt drive out the Canaanites, though they have iron chariots, and though they be strong."
In this scene Joshua was near the end of his years of leadership

of Israel and was parceling out the locations which were to be the inheritances of the various tribes. When Joshua came to the portion of the land which was to fall to the tribe of Joseph, he met some disapproval and resistance. The land given to them was narrow and wooded, and the people dwelling there who must be met were strong. Joshua took into account that those inhabitants of the land were a strong people, plus the fact that they had the advantage of machines of warfare which the tribe of Joseph did not possess. Joshua said that the tribe of Joseph would win the land though the Canaanites had iron chariots, which gave them a great advantage.

What Joshua said in the face of the unassailable fact of superior military force must have seemed like sheer folly to those who did not possess the faith in God which Joshua possessed. Look at the issue, examine the odds, consider the dangers, and any woman or man without faith is right in throwing up both hands in despair. Nathan Scott has written a book called *The Broken Center*. In it, Scott speaks of tragedy and the "tragic hero" who stands on some chill boundary of the world where all certainties have collapsed and all hope has disappeared. Now the person who is without Christian faith might easily come to that. Standing with Joshua, such a person must conclude that there is no way through, no way out, no deliverance, no escape, and no liberation. The Canaanites had chariots of iron, and on the ordinary form chart, in the regular reckoning, this made the case of the Israelites hopeless since they did not have chariots of iron.

God knows the world of sense and sound, of raw material power and bristling, bruising physical might, will chill you and terrify you if you have only physical eyes and, therefore, can see only physical things. There is much around us to intimidate, to discourage. Righteous God-fearing people cannot help noticing that in our society so many of the instruments of influence are in the hands of people who seem to care little about the things of our God and his Christ. For instance, what is spent to attend professional football games on one Sunday will embarrassingly dwarf the foreign mission budgets of many entire denominations.

What a futile life must anyone have who faces all of the uncertainties and imponderables of life with no resources of faith and vision of things unseen. The odds are all against us, and the hazards that are set against us are like "chariots of iron." Seeing the disappointments and the cloudy judgments with which we must proceed in so much of life, the physical dangers, and the psychic risks we must all take, it must seem often to many that we cannot bring life off with any honor or decency because we must fight against iron "chariots." The wonder is not that we men and women should be sometimes afraid, given the grim things which can leap up at us all of a sudden. The wonder is that we should ever be free of fear and terror if we are looking alone at what is visible and likely. It is not hard to prophesy what course each of our lives will follow. Take the case of your father, trace your mother's life in its main events, and you will have your own life. There will be some bright days, there will be many dull, gray days, there will be some storm-filled days, there will be sickness and separation, and at last there will be death. "Theses preachers make me sick with all their gloom," some say. Well, as a doctor friend of mine used to say long ago to his patients, "You do not want the truth: you want to be fooled."

They have iron chariots, but "you will overcome" is the word which Joshua spoke to the children of Joseph. Now, unless Joshua knew something which the surface evidence does not reveal, this is the saddest word in the world. Those that are against you have iron chariots, and you do not have chariots of iron, but you will drive them out. A reasonable person has the right to ask Joshua, "Sir, on what do you base your evidence?" What Joshua said to the children of Joseph was either cruel deception or the most ridiculous and groundless optimism, unless he was looking somewhere other than at the facts.

Well, the record is that this wild, incredible word which Joshua spoke to the tribe of Joseph did come to pass. The Canaanites with their chariots of iron and their strength did give way to the children of God's covenant. How could Joshua confidently say this to the tribe of Joseph and not be dealing in the most dangerous deception?

The answer to that question lies in what the prophet Elisha saw and what he prayed for his young companion to see: "LORD, I pray thee, open his eyes, that he may see. And the LORD opened the eyes of the young man; and he saw: and, behold, the mountain was full of horses and chariots of fire round about Elisha."

Elisha, servant of God, was being pursued by the Syrian king Benhadad because Elisha had revealed to Israel's king what the Syrian ruler was planning, and Israel had been saved on the principle of "to be forewarned is to be forearmed." Benhadad, seeing his secret plans foiled, had decided that there was a security leak. He thought somebody on his staff was letting the word get out, so his plans were known and thwarted by Israel.

Here is another place where "outsiders" to God will find understanding very difficult. Children will often think that someone has told their parents on them, as we say. Not necessarily so! People in a church will think sometimes that someone has been "running to the pastor," as some say. Not necessarily so! People will think that somebody has been "dipping in their business" and telling plans they have, which means someone is no good. Not necessarily so! God does get things to us in some way or another. He does put us on guard. He will reveal the things we need to know if we will but open ourselves to his Spirit.

Elisha told Israel's king each time, and finally Benhadad, the king of Syria, found out it was Elisha. He decided to get Elisha out of the way. Finding out that the prophet was staying in Dothan, Benhadad planned to set a trap by night. The king of Syria sent an order that a detachment of troops, horsemen, and chariots be dispatched to Dothan. They were ordered to march under the cover of darkness so the trap would be carefully set. Behold the Syrian army preparing for the march: the iron chariots stand in long, ominous rows; the foot soldiers stand rank on rank; the pawing horses with their ramrod straight riders are prancing. As night comes, the army of Syria bivouacs against one lone prophet. How strong the powers of evil seem, a "flood of mortal ills prevailing." Quietly, the army, the horsemen, the iron chariots of Syria, surround the town of Dothan.

Early the next morning, Elisha's young servant lad gets up, perhaps to prepare breakfast. He walks out of the home where Elisha is staying, and through his sleep-drowsed eyes he sees this strange sight. Everywhere he turns the lad sees the glint of swords, lances, and the great row of iron chariots surrounding the city. Enemy chariots and horses to the north, to the south, to the east, to the west — a ring of iron around a defenseless child of God. The young man cries to Elisha, "Alas, my master! how shall we do?" (v. 15).

It takes faith to answer that kind of question. Elisha said, "Fear not," a foolish word unless he knew something. "They that be with us are more than they that be with them" (v. 16). Then he prayed, "LORD, . . . open [the young man's] eyes." As the boy's eyes were opened, he saw the mountains full of horses and chariots of fire round about the hills. The young man saw not just rocks and vegetation but the armies of the living God, the fiery chariots of deliverance. A flaming ring of protection encircled the prophet. Chariots aflame signaled the power and presence of the Lord God Almighty.

Always around those who put their trust in God are keepers and guardians. Someone sings, "Angels keep watching over me." The messengers of God are all around us. They take different shapes according to the circumstances. When ringed by foes, these messengers of God become fiery chariots and horses pawing in their strength. When we are perplexed, these visitants become advisers and counselors to lead us into the truth. When we are sad and lonely, these messengers are comforters. Jesus said, "I will pray the Father, and he shall give you another Comforter" (John 14:16). Yes, angels do keep watching over us. Those with us are more than those against us.

> Who shall separate us from the love of Christ? shall tribulation, or distress, or persecution, or famine, or nakedness, or peril, or sword? . . . Nay, in all these things we are more than conquerors through him that loved us. For I am persuaded, that neither death, nor life, nor angels, nor principalities, nor powers, nor things present, nor things to come, Nor height, nor depth, nor any other creature, shall be able to separate us from the love of God, which is in Christ Jesus our Lord. (Romans 8:35,37–39)

∞ 12 ∞

A Christian Plan for Living

Philippians 3:13–14

Brethren, I count not myself to have apprehended: but this one thing I do, forgetting those things which are behind, and reaching forth unto those things which are before, I press toward the mark for the prize of the high calling of God in Christ Jesus. (Philippians 3:13–14)

I want to talk with you about "a Christian plan for living." My old college president Dr. J. A. Bacoats used to say, "It's better to fail with a plan than to succeed without one." I never quite understood that. As the years have come and gone, I have some better glimmer of it. One thing, if you fail with a plan, you know what to do. If you fail after you succeeded and did not have a plan, you do not know how you got there anyhow. We Christians need a plan for our lives. Let me read a passage of Scripture from the third chapter of Paul's letter to the church at Philippi. In the thirteenth and fourteenth verses of the third chapter of the letter which Paul wrote to the church at Philippi: "Brethren, I count not myself to have apprehended: but this one thing I do, forgetting those things which are behind, and reaching forth unto those things which are before, I press toward the mark for the prize of the high calling of God in Christ Jesus." When you think of who wrote that, it takes on new meaning.

Many times we feel that we have gone all out and we have served well. We have done what we should have done, and sometimes we feel we've done more than we should have done. The apostle Paul says, "I count not myself to have done what I should; I have not yet reached my goal." What a word when you think of who said that. You preach the gospel and serve Christ; you think you have gone beyond your own limit of endurance. Hear the apostle Paul say, "I count not myself to have reached my goal."

75

When you think about who said that, it ought to humble all of us. Paul wrote that he had been shipwrecked more than once in the cause of Jesus Christ and had spent a night and a day in the deep. Three times, he said, he received lashes, thirty-nine lashes. Once he was stoned at Lystra and turned up preaching the next day at Derbe, thirty miles away. And he says, "I count not myself to have reached my goal." What sacrifices have we made to compare with that? I would that our whole land could confess we are not yet what we ought to be.

Instead of making believe that we are the democracy that we are meant to become, instead of claiming that, if we could admit that we have not yet reached the level of freedom and democracy and opportunity for all of our people in this country, we would be a better people. We have been so slow to do so. We make believe that we have reached our goal. When we think of the plague of drugs which has spread through the land, which has so afflicted our own neighborhood, which has inflicted upon them so much damage, so much damage to our young people, we wonder why it is that a great nation like this cannot stop drugs from coming into our cities. We have the means and mechanisms by which we are able to not only gaze at the stars, but we have been able to put our foot upon the great planets of outer space. Yet we are not able to stop drugs from coming into America. We heard the other day that we were able to fire missiles into Iraq that could target particular aims, but we have not yet been able to find out from where the drugs come. And we have not been able to stop them from coming into this country. A great nation, not able to do that. We ought to confess that we have not yet reached our goal.

There are people in this country — and many of us may well agree with them — who feel that there ought not be a means of stopping life before it begins. Many people believe that, and I have no argument with it. But there are people in America who insist that children be born, and with that I have no argument. But once the children are born, these same people are willing to starve them to death. The same people who insist that the babies be born are willing through their national legislature to starve them. Do you find that a strange combination? We talk about pro-life while letting children starve to death. And if by chance they survive the starving, then execute them by the time they are grown, put them to death. They must be born, starve them, and then put them to death, and that is called pro-life. We need to confess that we have not yet reached the goal for which this nation was begun. "I count not myself to have apprehended." All Christians, each one of us, ought to make that confession, that we have not yet reached what we ought to be. Do you know that you are able to think God's thoughts and to walk, so to speak, in the footsteps of God? Yet when we look around at our own lives, we discover how short of that we are.

Jesus said that we have within us the capacity to order that a mountain be moved and it will commit suicide in the sea. But our prayer life is so weak that we are unable to influence our communities and to bring about changes in our neighborhoods and in our own households. We ought to confess that we have not yet apprehended, we have not yet reached our goal, we have not yet put our hands upon that for which we have been ordained. With all of the enthusiasm we see around us, would you not say that we have scarcely begun to be what the Lord wants us to be? We have hardly learned the alphabet of grace, to say nothing of the language of salvation. So far behind are we poor faltering, stumbling, meandering, fretful creatures. And we ought to be strong in Jesus Christ, able to turn back the powers of darkness. We have not yet reached our goal. It is very possible that a truly praying person could change all of this town. A praying congregation might change all of America. We have not yet apprehended that for which we have already had hands laid on us.

So Paul says that, and I would to God that black people could confess that we have not yet reached what we should have reached in terms of our background. Do you not know that black people have gone through great trials in this country and have suffered unimaginable indignities and outrages? And yet we who are their heirs find ourselves far weaker than they were with all of the disadvantages that they had, with all of the mountains that they had to climb, with all of the difficulties that they had to overcome. Here we are with all of the advantages we have and all of the opportunities that we have, and we have not yet reached what we should have been, what we should have been a long time ago. I count not myself to have apprehended that for which I have already been apprehended. And if here on this day there would be people who would be saying to themselves, "I am willing, God, to be whatever you want me to be; I am willing to climb whatever hill, whatever mountain; I am willing to travel whatever road you would have me; I am ready," the Lord could do great things with us.

I have preached now for fifty years. As I look back upon that, I remember that I have not been near what I might have been if my prayer life had been deeper and more sincere. If my heart had been more open to the things of God, so much more, so infinitely much more, could have been done. Do you look at your life, as I look at mine, and say, "I have not yet apprehended that for which I have been apprehended"? I have not yet reached my goal. I have not yet laid claim upon my possession in Jesus Christ. I have not yet won my right to be called a child of God. I count not myself to have apprehended.

Paul says that, and we marvel...Here was a man who had been lashed several times, spent a night and a day in the deep, was shipwrecked, lost family, friends. You read Paul's writings, and you will read maybe one or two small references to some cousin or some aunt or some other relative, but nothing about his family back in Tarsus. I found out from someone preaching up at Brown University, one of the New Testament scholars, that a Jew of Paul's time found his or her being, her sense of significance or his sense of significance, by being a part of a family. And yet this man says nothing about his family. You know why? Because very likely they had disowned him. He had turned to Jesus Christ, and they wanted no more to do with him. He had spent twenty-five or thirty years wandering up and down the empire, sometimes missing ships, sometimes getting into towns late at night and not knowing where he would stay, sometimes being criticized by enemies of the church, sometimes being criticized by people in the church, because our problem is not only on the outside but is also on the inside. Paul says, "I count not myself." Amazing! Now who are we? What sacrifices have we made? What spiritual power can we claim when this man said with all that he had sacrificed, with all he had given up, "I have not yet..."? That's the first thing we need to do.

"But this one thing I do, forgetting those things which are behind." How we need to turn toward the future. Ah, in this country, we in our great black communities of America need to stop saying to our young people that slavery is holding them back. There is some truth there. We ought to say it to other people, but we ought not say it to ourselves. I was born fifty-odd years after slavery; I knew people who had passed through the dark night of slavery. They came out of the awful servitude with the stench of their enslavement in their garments. They came out and started schools, they started churches, and they began groceries and insurance companies. We are one hundred years later saying that slavery has held us back. There is truth in that which the nation ought to recognize and rectify, but we black people ought to rid ourselves of feelings of weakness. We need to put that behind us and march on to what God has in store for us, forgetting those things which are behind.

Paul says in his final word, "I press toward the mark." There are people who claim that our Christian witness is a kind of weak, bloodless, helpless, fragile, faltering, staggering kind of thing. But do you catch the vigor? Do you catch the fire, catch the determination? "I press"; that's not a relaxed word. You can almost see the sweat standing out on the brow, so to speak. "I press." The veins are sticking out. Here is a man under great strength of purpose. "I press toward the mark."

I ask you, do you know what the mark of the high calling is? Christians, do you know what you have before you, everyone of us? I almost hesitate even to mention; it sounds so vast and so far beyond us. But did you know that you are destined as a child of God one day to become so much like Jesus Christ that angels looking at one another and looking at you and looking at Jesus might ask one another, "Which one is Jesus?" For does the New Testament not say, "It does not yet appear what we shall be, but this we know that when he shall appear we shall be like him"? Like him, for we shall see him as he is. So Paul says, "I press," sometimes up, sometimes down, sometimes almost level with the ground. But I press toward the mark, sometimes feeble, sometimes failing, sometimes weeping, sometimes discontent, but I press toward the mark. Sometimes in good report, sometimes in evil report, but I press toward the prize.

Do you press? I say to you today that I know what it is to have great sorrow. I know what it is not to know which way you are going sometimes. I know what it is to dampen the pillow some nights with one's own tears. I even know what it is to hope almost against hope not to wake up the next morning. Life can be very difficult. But press on! Today the battle shout, tomorrow the victor's song. Press on! We're bound for Emmanuel's land, where sickness and sorrow and pain and death are felt and feared no more. Press on! There's a bright side somewhere; don't you rest until you find it. Press on! God's mercy stoops low, and his pity bows down to help us. Press on! Press on! Our eyes may be wet with tears sometimes, but the promise is that God shall wipe away all tears from our eyes. Press on! Your salvation is nearer than when you first began. God wrought it; Christ brought it; the Holy Spirit taught it. Praise God my soul caught it!

∽ 13 ∾

The Christian Response to Trouble

Acts 8:4

Therefore they that were scattered abroad went every where preaching the word. (Acts 8:4)

What I am talking about this morning is something which all of us must deal with from the earliest of our time in the earth to almost the latest breath we draw. Well, I say you've got to deal with it. Long years ago, one of our deacons, Hamilton Stark, was one of the custodians of Concord Church. Whenever he was told that there was something he had to do, he would say, "Ain't got to do nothing but die." Well I say, you've got to deal with *this,* but maybe I had better acknowledge that there is an exception. There is a city where you're free of it. The people in it do not have mailing addresses, but they have headstones. If you want to be free from what I'm talking about, that is the city for you. Nobody there will trouble you, nothing there will trouble you, and God knows you will not trouble anybody. Now if you don't want that, then you've got to take what I'm talking about this morning. *Trouble* belongs to all of us!

You can deal with difficulty in several ways. You can shrug your shoulders and say, "It's the roll of the dice; it's the way it happens. It's the rub of the green; it's the bounce of the ball." But deal with it you must.

I ought to say that what I going to talk about is aimed at Christian people. There is a hazy universalism which some of us want to believe in, that whatever the Lord says, he is saying it to everybody. He is saying it to everybody who qualifies. I know of no promise that the Lord Jesus has made to everybody. Everybody is eligible, but everybody does not necessarily qualify. Do you get the difference between being eligible and qualifying? He says,

"Fear not, little flock [not everybody]; it is the Father's good pleasure to give you the kingdom." He says, "Whosoever believeth should not perish." He says, the New Testament says, "All things work together for good to them that love God."

You're eligible, but you've got to qualify. And anybody here this morning can qualify, and I hope to God if you have not qualified, being eligible you won't pass up the opportunity to qualify. God has a plan for your life if you are within covenant relationship with God. *Covenant relationship* means contract relationship. *Contract relationship* means an agreement between parties. If you are in covenant relationship with God, he has a plan for your life. He has a plan for your life even if you are not in covenant relationship, but the plan cannot be operative until you accept your part in the covenant. If God has a plan for your life and you will not accept your part in the contractual relationship he proposes, then the contract is null and void, of no effect, nonbinding! On the other hand, if you are in covenant relationship, God has a plan for your life. He has a plan that trouble cannot conquer. If you are in covenant relationship with God, he has a plan for your life, and all the devils in hell cannot defeat it. They may thwart, they may delay, they may impede, they may annoy, they may irritate, but they cannot defeat God's plan for your life. If you are in covenant relationship, they cannot prevail.

Listen to this word: "Therefore they that were scattered abroad went every where preaching the word." This sounds very simple, but a great deal hides in those simple words. The little church was in Jerusalem; that is where it started. The last time I talked to you, I talked about how the resurrected Lord said to his fearful people, "Tarry in Jerusalem, until you be endued with power," and they did. I then tried to talk to you about how the mighty inrushing wind and indwelling Spirit came upon them and transformed them from a defeated, bedraggled people into radiant, glorious, triumphant heralds of their risen Lord — afraid of nobody. People who had been cringing in corners walked boldly to public places and began talking about what the Lord had done for them in Jesus Christ. The inspired disciples were in Jerusalem and happy. Jerusalem was where the church had begun. It was there that the baptism of fire came upon them and transformed them. They were familiar with Jerusalem. They knew its streets; they had friends there. It was a congenial atmosphere. They knew how to operate, and perhaps they would have stayed there, for it was territory that they could handle. They were at home there, they had connections, and they had the memory of how the Holy Spirit had come down upon them, like cloven tongues of fire, and settled upon them until fear came out of them. A great faith and confidence had come into their hearts and into their lives. This was their city, but trouble came. The New Testament says that when trouble came, it changed their situation.

Christians, when trouble comes, we all turn into a momentary panic. I think it takes a saint, maybe more than a saint, not to be jolted, staggered, when something happens that looks bad. You say, "My God, my God," but a Christian ought not linger in panic. Panic is the mood that belongs to somebody that does not have a way out! That's what panic is all about. If there is nothing you know to do and you do not see a way out, then you are likely to go into a panic. But the moment you have a plan, panic has no power over you. Panic operates where paralysis has taken place, where the mind is confused, where you just break into a cold sweat because there doesn't look like there is any way out. But the Christian has a way out when trouble comes. The first thing a Christian ought to remember is that God has a plan. You may not understand it clearly, but God has a plan.

If trouble had not broken out in Jerusalem, if persecution had not come to rest upon that little church, if the authorities had not turned on them, the church would have stayed there. I might not be preaching here this morning, and you might not be sitting here if the church had been allowed to stay in Jerusalem. But trouble came. And when trouble comes, the first thing a Christian ought to remember is that God has a plan. God is not trapped; he's not baffled; he's not without resources.

A lot of things are happening in this country now, but God has a plan. I do not know what it is, but I think sometimes I see clearly. There continues in this nation a great furor which rages about affirmative action. One cannot escape the conclusion that those of us who favor affirmative action have been inept in allowing the main emphasis to be placed on race rather than gender. The opponents of affirmative action said very little about the advantages that policy brings to women who have been discriminated against because of their gender. That aspect of affirmative action has been downplayed in order not to arouse the tremendous voting strength of the women of America. Sadly enough, women seem to have fallen into the trap as well. Ponder that! Still, God has a plan. In this whole matter of cutting back on civil rights and affirmative action, God has a plan. While I continue saying to the majority culture, "You have done wrong and ought to do something about it," I will also continue to say to black people that if nobody does something about it, we must do something about it, among ourselves. We must learn to read and write and figure and match other people and compete in this society. And we can do it. If our black preachers, black teachers, black leaders, will tell us the truth and tell us to stand on our feet and hold our heads high, and then do whatever it takes to match wits with anybody. We can make it; we can make it! God has a plan.

My friend Vernon Jordan spoke in Atlanta last week and sent me a copy of the draft. He said that what people — and he's right — what people are contending for in China and in other places in parts of the world is democracy. They are contending for what we say we have. What they want is something better that what they've got now, and if you want to know the truth, better than what *we've* got. They're not contending for a divided nation, divided according to class, with a great deal of poverty and poor health and poor education. They are contending for what we claim we have. And the less we live up to what we claim, the more hypocritical the rest of the world will see us. God has a plan, make no mistake; he moves in a mysterious way, his wonders to perform, plants his footsteps upon the sea, and really rides upon every storm.

So when trouble came in the city of Jerusalem, the church was scattered abroad. As they had to leave, forced out of the city, as they went, they went talking about Jesus, and the gospel moved out. It was Alexander Maclaren who said that the violent hand of persecution turns out to be that hand which scattered the seed of the gospel to the ends of the earth. That's exactly what happened. The enemies of Christ were routing people out of their homes and forcing them to leave the city, so everywhere they went they were talking about Jesus, how the Lord had lifted them. As they went, they found out that the Lord would take care of them wherever they went. We do not find out when things are going well with us how well the Lord will see about us. We find out when trouble comes how well the Lord will take care of us. We find out in dark days how the Lord's light will shine on our pathways. We find out in the storms that he is our refuge and our hiding place in the tempest. We find out when the drought of life comes upon us that he is a river of water in dry places and the shadow of a great rock in a weary land.

We do not like things to happen to us which we consider unfavorable. Still we are called on to face something or the other which hurts us and hampers us. In every such circumstance, we must remember that we are not in this business of living by ourselves. There is another who walks the sunnied and shadowed ways of life with us, and when we do our best and our best is not good enough, he makes up the difference. God has a plan. Remember that it takes winter to make springtime and remember that God turns stumbling blocks into stepping stones and remember that God can turn any midnight into daybreak. Never forget that God can make a way when there is no way. Remember that God can do whatever your soul needs to have done. God can bring peace out of every confusion. God can help the helpless. God can pick up the downtrodden. God can feed the hungry. God can help the helpless. Never forget it.

There are many things that you do not understand now. I don't know whether I ever told you this, but I must. My father died when I was turning thirteen. I cannot tell you how large he was in my eyes. I can testify now that the Lord has worked it out. As

I look back, I can see that I would've depended too much on him and on his reputation. Our old church building was destroyed by fire. I see now that the Lord was opening before us an infinitely large opportunity for service.

There are still some mysteries in my life, as there must be in yours. But I tell you what I believe. I believe that one day when the fog has lifted.... Because now we see through a glass darkly, it's hazy. But one day when the mist has rolled away, one day when we rise out of the mesmerism of nearsightedness, one day when the balances are struck, one day when it's all cleared up, one day when the line is struck and all the figures are added up, one day when we have passed through our sorrow, one day when we've drunk our last cup of sorrow, one day when trouble is behind us, one day when we rise above our weakness, one day when heaven comes permanently our souls to greet and glory forever crowns the mercy seat — one day we'll understand it better by and by. And one day we shall thank the Lord; we shall thank him. Thank him for every tear, thank him for every fear, thank him for every sorrow, thank him for every trial, thank him for every tear, thank him for every sickness. We'll understand it better; yes we will. Better, better, by and by. We cannot see it clearly now, but one day....

$\backsim$ 14 $\backsim$

A City with Other Walls

Zechariah 2:3–5

And, behold, the angel that talked with me went forth, and another angel went out to meet him, And said unto him, Run, speak to this young man, saying, Jerusalem shall be inhabited as towns without walls for the multitude of men and cattle therein: For I, saith the LORD, will be unto her a wall of fire round about, and will be the glory in the midst of her. (Zechariah 2:3–5)

On a flight to Dallas, some years ago, I happened to sit next to a man who was a securities lawyer in that city. In explaining that Dallas is a city that has become a major metropolis without any geographical advantage, this gentleman pointed out that almost every city of any note is founded on the water. This is true surely of most of the old and best-known cities — London, Paris, Rome, Tokyo — and once in many ways, the most wonderful of them all — New York. The reason is obvious: in past times the movement of cargo depended almost completely on waterways — seas and rivers.

Perhaps the next thing in importance to how cargo would be brought in and would get out was the question of protection. Great cities are not naturally safe places. The major danger was once attack from an outside enemy. Thus the cities of antiquity had walls surrounding them. Tourists in foreign countries will often see segments and ruins of these ancient walls still standing. These walls, now brown with age, contained gates through which travelers and trade passed to and fro.

Among the most notable of these walls of protection is that guarding more than a city. It is the wall that guarded much of the Chinese border and is called the Great Wall of China. This wall stands thirty feet high and is broad enough to accommodate a column of soldiers. Such is its magnitude that it has been dubbed one of the Seven Wonders of the Middle Ages. It was built as a defense against invaders. I shall come back to this last statement later.

The speaker of our text, Zechariah, prophesied at the time when Jerusalem was being rebuilt following the great national calamity of 587 B.C., when foreigners overcame the Holy City and carried her sons and daughters away as slaves. This tremendous reversal of fortune gave rise to one of the most plaintive laments known to human history, as the former sons and daughters of Jerusalem pondered the pain and heartbreak of their plight by the bayous and canals that ran through the land of their captivity. In a home-sick tone they said, "By the rivers of Babylon we sat down and we wept when we remembered Jerusalem. They that carried us captive required of us a song. But how can we sing the songs of the Lord in a strange land?" (Psalm 137:1–4, *paraphrased*).

In our text, the national humiliation is over, since all things — good and bad — do pass away. Life is an uneven journey, as we have said often. Life is, in a way, a wheel, and if you stay on it and are down, you will surely rise. The captivity is past; there has been a radical shift in international politics. At this point the prophet Zechariah speaks of the vision of a young man who has a measuring rod in his hand and who seems on his way to do some measuring. Where is he going? To measure the dimensions of the city with a view to laying out a plan for building a wall of protection around the city. No more invaders. No more being carried away to weep. No more being caught unawares.

We all want to protect some cities of our affections, be they group or individual interests. We want to protect our feelings against betrayal and so are loathe to make friends and trust others. It would be unreasonable to suggest that we ought not to try to protect our interests. Such advice would be credited to coming from fools. At the same time, we can never really protect and shield our interests and our loves in such a way that they are to-tally safe. No wall ascends high enough, extends wide enough, or is planted deep enough to permit this. Let me use our children as an example. We want to protect our children and thereby some-times overprotect them, either driving them from us in the process or rendering them too weak and flabby to take their places in the rough give-and-take of life's struggle. You have to turn them loose if they are ever going to make it.

Some of you may recall the old preaching theme of our black forebears on the subject of the eagle stirring her nest. That account, taken from Deuteronomy, told how the mother eagle senses when the eaglets have been in the aerie, that strange word for the eagle's nest, too long. She takes them one by one on her back and flies out at dizzying height, up amidst the craggy summits and snow-covered peaks of the surrounding mountains. Then she swoops and unseats her little riders, and they, frightened, scream, but instinctively they call on their own gift of flight. If they fall too far, the mother dips beneath them and supports and sustains them, only to repeat the same procedure, until the eaglets soar as eagles are born to soar.

So with our children! If I may go back to the symbol in our text, we cannot build a wall around them. We also cannot build walls around our husbands and wives — or even ourselves. We have read of a man of great wealth who died some years ago and who spent fantastic amounts of money to shield himself from contact with germs. It became a sickness, apparently. Still, he died. Surely, we ought to take reasonable precautions, but to become a hypochondriac, always believing ourselves afflicted with any disease of which we hear, is a greater sickness than that which we fear.

In the new millennium we ought to realize that in all of our human relations and in our mortal journey we, when all is said and done, are really helpless creatures. We can do little to protect, so little to defend, others and ourselves. This is true too of other things that are dear to our hearts. Many of us love our churches, but we cannot keep people from saying ugly things about them. Minority people have heroically struggled in this land and against great odds. We would that people would appreciate and applaud such gallantry. Still there are those in America who unfailingly discount and sneer at minority communities. We realize that a wall cannot be erected to prevent bigots on television and elsewhere from downplaying and discounting unbelievable achievements of survival by a people.

How shall we defend ourselves? In this new millennium, we need to understand this about spiritual undertakings and about spiritually minded people. Spiritually motivated enterprises cannot fight with the same weapons that are used by those who are carnally minded, self-oriented, flesh-bound, and hell-bent. Their weapons are prohibited to God's called and chosen people. The world's methods of lying, cheating, slandering, plotting, and manipulating are areas closed to a child of God and follower of Jesus. But this does not mean that God's people are defenseless. This does not mean that the Lord's followers are without protection.

Let the word go forth that whoever touches harmfully the "Lord's anointed," the Lord's anointed work, the Lord's anointed purposes, touches with ugly and destructive hands the Omnipotent himself. God will defend and if necessary destroy. I would rather my hand be cut off than that it raise itself against the Lord's purposes. I would rather this tongue was plucked out of the mouth than that it be employed to try to block the purposes of the everlasting God. God's purposes will ripen fast, unfolding every hour.

This is a new circumstance; this is a time when we are commanded to stand still and see the salvation of the Lord. Better still, while we do the best we can with the weapons we have — our minds, our experience, our judgments, our gifts, denied the world's tools, the Lord will make perfect that which concerneth us.

Zechariah tells us in contemplation of the new city of Jerusalem that walls were not intended to be its defense. A city without walls — this was a strange concept since cities without walls were unknown in antiquity. It is only in recent times by the creation of large countries with common interests that cities have been built without physical walls. There is a splendid audacity in the thought that the new city will have no walls.

Might it be that the prophet was really trying to say that man-made defenses never defend, are never enough, that we need more? If this was the idea, practical, political history bears him out. The Great Wall of China, wide enough for a column of soldiers to stand upon, was breached. Someone bribed a gatekeeper, and an army poured in — so runs an ancient account. We cannot protect our dearest treasures; we cannot stay the hand of disease nor prevent the swift blows of accidents to those we love and whose good estate is our deepest earthly hope. Even those we love must take their blows, face their temptations, and weep their tears.

I tell you what we can do! We can ask the Lord for fulfillment of the old promise, and we can lean upon it. Just lean. Zechariah said, "The Lord will be a wall of fire round about the city." We can ask the Lord to be a wall around our loved ones, our people, our nation, and our world. We can't do it ourselves. The devil is ever vigilant; his wiles and tricks are legion. But we can commit ourselves to God for safekeeping. Lord, be a wall of fire around us. Lord, as another millennium settles in, when the enemy swiftly rides forth with weapons that annul, assassinate, and annihilate, Lord, be a wall of fire around us.

"The angel of the LORD encampeth round about them that fear him" (Psalm 34:7). "[They] that dwelleth in the secret place of the most high shall abide under the shadow of the Almighty" (Psalm 91:1). "For he shall give his angels charge over thee, to keep thee in all thy ways. They shall bear thee up in their hands" (Psalm 91:11). Above all, the living Lord, our risen, reigning, returning Savior says, "Lo, I am with you always, even unto the end of the world" (Matthew 28:20).

May the Lord keep you in the hollow of his hand. May he defend you from enemies seen and unseen and escort you from perilous danger. May the protector of the poor and the defender of the weak safeguard your going out and your coming in. May the Lord keep you every day.

> May the God of hosts
> Keep your heart, and keep your hand,
> Keep your soul, I pray.
> Keep your tongue to speak God's praise,
> Keep thee all the way.

༄ 15 ༄

ENOUGH GOD

Mark 4:37–39

And there arose a great storm of wind, and the waves beat into the ship, so that it was now full. And he was in the hinder part of the ship, asleep on a pillow: and they awake him, and say unto him, Master, carest thou not that we perish? And he arose, and rebuked the wind, and said unto the sea, Peace, be still. And the wind ceased, and there was a great calm. (Mark 4:37–39)

I'm talking this morning about having no God, having a counterfeit god, having half gods, and having enough God. One of the occupational hazards of the work I do, as I have said to you many times in many ways, is nervousness before the time of speaking or preaching. One of the most anxious of my times occurred before my first lecture at Harvard University. I thought of the venerable reputation of that oldest of our American schools, all of that. The lecture was to be in the old chapel of the Harvard Divinity School. On the wall to your left as one stands facing those he or she speaks to are the words of Ralph Waldo Emerson in his commencement address of, I think, 1838, or there about. On the first line from that address of his is the exhortation "Acquaint thyself with deity." Of course, one of the criticisms of Emerson and those New England transcendentalists, as they were called, was that their sense of God was not as close and personal and intimate, at least as they expressed it, as some of us would like. But acquaint thyself with deity, with God.

I raise the question this morning, What God? for there are many people traveling the road of life. . . . Do I address myself this morning to one or some of them? There are many people who have for their object of worship — for that is what a god is, an object of worship — who have for their god a counterfeit, a fake deity. I suppose that there is no letdown in life so dreadful as having clasped to oneself, held on to, what we believe was a savior and then in some critical hour when time is too far gone to ever get it back to find out we have been duped....Oh, I have no right to stand here and say that there's ever a time when we cannot make a change and cannot, so to speak, get it back, but you understand me. What a dreadful thought it must be to hold on to some object of worship and to believe that in whatever circumstance I might find myself this that I worship will sustain me and hold me and then in a moment when there's no chance to regroup, you see, no time to reorganize and to reorder the arrangement, because there are times in life when we do not have opportunity to, as we say, get ourselves together, when there's no opportunity to regroup and to reorganize and in that moment to discover what we thought would hold us gives way. That must be an awful experience. Many of us have fake gods.

Read when you go home, will you, the forty-sixth chapter of the book of Isaiah, where the prophet is making fun of, ridiculing, people who have fake gods. Back in that day it was an actual figure that they set up. They bowed down before it; they prayed to it; they made offerings before it. And the prophet is laughing about this, in a more or less holy laugh, I take it. He is saying, "Here is what you do." And do not think these people were so old-fashioned when I will have described them. Apply them, let us apply them, to ourselves. He said that you go with a bag. You pull out some gold, and you give it to a goldsmith. You ask him to make you a god: "Make me something that I can worship, an object of my adoration and of my reverence, that I can turn to, that I can feel comforted in the presence of, that I believe will give me a feeling of well-being; make me a god." He does. He makes the god, and then you put the god there before you. But when you get ready to go to another place — read that forty-sixth chapter, for it is one of the great ironies recorded in the Scripture — you've got to pick up your god. If the wind blows too hard, your god falls over, and you've got to put your god back up straight. And when you get ready to go from one place to the other, you've got to take your god and put your god on your shoulder and carry your god somewhere else, where you'll put your god down and bow down. Well, any god you've got to carry is not worth being called a god. As a matter of fact, if you've got to carry your god, then you're more god than your god is. I think that is the test of whether anything, or anybody for that matter, is worth being a god: whether you've got to carry it or him or her, however you want to put it. If you are doing the transporting, you don't have a real god; you have a fake, a counterfeit god, a god that's not real. Bow down before it, adore it, worship it, praise it, revere it, honor it, but you are honoring a counterfeit.

Now Ralph Waldo Emerson, whom I quoted a moment ago, in some writings spoke of half gods. They are not altogether fake, but they are not full gods. I don't know which is worse: to have no god or a half god. The half god can do something for you, but not what you need. A professor out in one of the California universities has this week released a finding about our young people in college. It says that our young people for the last eight years have been primarily concerned with what they are going to make when they get out, what status they are going to have, what promotions they are going to get, and how they are going to make it in life. They are concerned, so the California research person says, with what they are going to make. We in this country are so eaten up with our technologies and our know-how. The truth of the matter in our country is that we worship our machinery and our chrome-plated technology; that's what we worship. And that's why our young people are like that. They did not start it; they got it from their elders. But we have lost so much in this country about ideals, about justice, about truths, and about righteousness. I'm coming back one more time, and I hope not to come back to it again, about these old, these old, hearings about Iran. Many things came out of those hearings about Iran-Contra and our participation in corruption. One is that in our country great numbers of people are not concerned about truth, about justice, about honor, about democracy, about the Constitution.

I knew a man when I was in graduate school; he was an older man, and he had come back to study. He had a shiny new, I can see it now, blue Buick automobile, 1937 — a pretty thing. He would dust it every morning; this is the truth. And he would not only dust it, but he would change clothes to dust his car. Every evening, he would change clothes and go out and dust his car. If it rained, the rain could hardly stop before he was out getting the rain off, half damp and wet himself, getting the rain off his shiny new car, a half god. We are so taken with know-how, but not with "know-what" or "know-why" or "know-whom." But I say to you that a god who is only know-how is not a god; that's a half god. A whole god must produce for us a know-how, a know-what, a know-why, *and* a know-whom. Right there is Jesus Christ.

Now let me read my text. I knew I was going to get to this text before I finished:

> And there arose a great storm of wind, and the waves beat into the ship, so it was now full. And he was in the hinder part of the ship, asleep on a pillow: and they awake him, and say unto him, Master, carest thou not that we perish? And he arose, and rebuked the wind, and said unto the sea, Peace, be still. And the wind ceased, and there was a great calm.

Now I'll tell you right off what enough God is. Enough God is a god who can get low enough to reach you and me and to understand who we are, what we are, and where we are. We cannot use a god who cannot get close enough to us to be able to take our pulse and understand what our condition is. It may be a wonderful grand deity, but there is no practical value to me if my god cannot understand where I am and what I am. If my god can understand what I am and who I am and where I am and cannot do anything about it, I don't have enough God. What we have to have is a God with power and with tenderness, a God most wonderfully kind, and a God almighty. If you can't get to where I am, you can't do anything for me. If my god doesn't understand my tears and my heartbreak, my grief, my longings, my aspirations, it's very little, no matter how powerful he might be, that he can do for me. If he understands my thoughts afar off and he knows my downsitting and my uprising and he can't do anything about it, he's not enough God for me.

The disciples are with Jesus Christ. They have traveled; they have crossed the waters; they have gone over as evening has come. He has spent a long day in healing and helping, in teaching and preaching. His body is weary and tired; exhaustion has set in. And as the ship crosses the Sea of Galilee, he lies down in the hinder part of the ship, the aft, as the naval people call it. In the hinder part of the ship he takes a pillow, and there on the rude boards of that ship with only a pillow to cushion him, he sleeps. Mary's child sleeps. He's weary, tired, exhausted. His strength has given out, and he sleeps. Sleeps because he has been doing the Father's work, sleeps because his conscience is clear, and sleeps because he's tired. A great number of people — I do not say all of them — but a great number of people who take sleeping pills do so because they have consciences which won't let them rest. You want a prescription for sleeping well? Treat people right. Try to help people as you go along the way. Don't dig ditches for other people; try to encourage them. Don't look on the dark side and the low side of everything. Look at things positively; look at your friends and at your family in a positive way. Don't always suspect the worst motives in other people; give them the benefit of the doubt, as you would like them to give you the benefit of the doubt. When evening comes, you can lie down with a calm conscience and sleep well.

I believe, for that matter, that in life's last evening you can sleep death's sleep much more easily if you have not mistreated people and have not gone around trying to hurt and bruise people and make them feel badly, and to pull them down and reduce them. I'm glad that Jesus was wearied, for it means that he has some identification with my condition when I am weary and exhausted, when I've got no more strength to give, when I'm at the edge of my resources, of my physical and emotional resources. He can understand because he got tired.

There are other instances of that weariness. It happens again and again in the Scriptures. Jesus was weary on that day when he sat by Jacob's well up in Samaria because he was thirsty, when he asked a woman to give him water. Strong Son of God, but Mary's baby. And then I can never read that account at Bethany at Lazarus's tomb without a strange emotion crossing me. I watch the Savior make his way to the grave of his friend. How would he stand there — aloof, separated as if what has happened to Lazarus and his family is some strange and alien event which cannot touch him? How will he react? When I see him standing there weeping, as the word stands in the New Testament, great convulsive sobs rack his body. He weeps. You know, that verse is the shortest verse in the New Testament, but it is one of the greatest verses in the New Testament when it tells us that the Lord Jesus, the Christ of God, is able to understand us. Don't you ever just read quickly and pass over, as if they don't count, those two words. "Jesus wept." Oh, no! That says more to me than simple words. Jesus wept. His heart was hurt; it ached; he knew sorrow, the pain of grief, and what it means to be separated from somebody you love. Thank God for that. Does Jesus care? Oh yes! I look at him at Lazarus's tomb with awe. The Son of God with tears flowing down his cheek, his whole body trembling under the impact of his deep emotion — so seeing, my heart finds hope and my fears about the eternal are assuaged.

So he slept. But then a great storm came. Winds became furious. Waves began chasing each other like wild horses. Lightning began in that evening sky, dancing nimbly across the face of the heavens. Great and ominous clouds hung low. The disciples on board the ship became agitated and then afraid. Many of them were seamen, so it was no ordinary storm. They had seen many a storm on the Sea of Galilee, but none like that. The great thunder drums roared; the lightning flashed; the winds roared; the waves frothed like mad dogs. The disciples came to him, "Master, Master, the tempest is raging, the billows are tossing high. Carest thou not that we perish?"

Jesus got up from his sleep, weary like I am, but able to do what I cannot do, what no half god can do, and what no counterfeit god can ever do. He got up, rubbed the cobwebs out of his eyes, and leaned over to the roaring sea. I wonder how he spoke. I've asked myself many times, did his voice rise above the thunder? Did it roar like the morning of creation? How did he speak? Or did he speak quietly because he knew he was in control? Did he speak calmly and quietly to the angry sea, to the agitated winds, to the flashing lightning, to the peals of thunder? Did he whisper to them, "Peace, peace, peace be still"?

The wind heard the Savior's voice and ran back to its hiding place in the hills. The rolling thunder came to mute silence. The lightning turned out its electricity. The great army of clouds lost their frown. "Peace, be still. Peace, winds, be quiet. Peace, thunder, be silent. Peace, lightning, flash no more, peace." The waves stretched humbly at his feet.

"Peace." That's a God enough to be able to understand my heartbreak and able to meet my needs. I know that he can speak peace. He spoke peace to my troubled soul, wrote my name in the Lamb's fair Book of Life. And now as I draw closer, I have confidence that he can make old Jordan be still. Asks the prophet, "what will you do in the swelling of Jordan?" Well, you know, I've reached a place now where I can hear the echo of Jordan in my ear. But I believe that when I come down to the river, he'll say to it, "Peace, let the purchase of my blood pass through."

∽ 16 ∾

THE EVERYWHERENESS OF GOD

Psalm 139:7–8

Whither shall I go from thy spirit? or whither shall I flee from thy presence? If I ascend up into heaven, thou art there: if I make my bed in hell, behold, thou art there. (Psalm 139:7–8)

I want to confront your hearts and minds with the subject "the everywhereness of God." Now, you need not arch your eyebrows at that word *everywhereness*. It will not intimidate me. For the last forty-five years, my landlady has been an affirmative-action-free, Oberlin College Phi Beta Kappa in language, so my pulpit speech has been subjected to all of the scrutiny to which it can be liable. As a matter of fact, when I mentioned to her that I wanted to talk about the "everywhereness" of God sometime ago, she admitted the possibility of such a word but raised serious questions about its respectability. I now baptize it and ordain it.

As that sublime hymn which we call the one hundredth and thirty-ninth psalm begins, we are treated to the musing of the poet as he reflects upon our lack of privacy before God: "Thou hast searched me, and known me. Thou knowest my downsitting and mine uprising, thou understandeth my thoughts afar off." We may thank God we have privacy from each other. My mother in the long ago used to say, "I know what you're thinking." Well thank goodness she did not know *all* that I was thinking. What a dreadful thing it would be if everyone here knew everything you have been thinking for the last two hours. We enjoy, thank God, a privacy one from the other, but we do not before God. Our forebear Adam found that to be, as he was paraded out in his exposed circumstance. But thank God we have privacy from each other. One of the great boons of a continuing marriage is another room into which one can walk, not aggressively, but tactfully, when things become too tense in the room in which one

99

has been. And, if I may pass out after all of these years some homespun advice, one of the great skills of continuing marriage is knowing when to go into the next room.

When our poet has dealt with our lack of privacy, he then begins to talk about the everywhereness of God: "Whither shall I go from thy spirit?" When Israel took its trek from Egypt to Canaan, its pilgrimage toward its grand and tragic experiment in nationhood, the people passed along the borders of many people and beheld gods held in reverence by many of those by the edges of whose lands they passed. They were referred to as local deities. They had territorial sovereignty. They were effective on their own turf, but beyond their borders they lacked authority. It was one of the most daring flights of the human spirit in all of history when the people of Israel in that long-ago day first declared that the God they served, and we serve, is without territorial boundaries, that he is not restricted by any geography. I said it was a flight of the human spirit. Perhaps more accurately, it was one of the most sublime visitations which humanity has ever known when that insight came to rest upon ancient Israel and came to inform their national life on through the centuries: "Whither shall I flee from thy presence? If I ascend up into heaven, thou art there."

There is a crude scientism still aboard in the world, though not as widely admitted now as it was in the days of my youth. It was begun really, I suppose, by Isaac Newton with his idea of God of the gaps. It was the theory that awe and reverence might exist wherever science had not planted its flag. To an early generation, reverence and ignorance were close kin. But as science pushed back the frontiers of our ignorance, God was forced to flee ever in advance of that onslaught. He was, so to speak, like a mountain animal driven from crag to crag until the last, when in some remote area of the universe he waited to be evicted even from that by the onrush of scientific inquiry. Rubbish! To discover something is not to create it. To read something is not to write it.

When the Russian cosmonauts first invaded outer space, they said that out in the far distances of the universe they saw no sign of God whatsoever. Tommy rot. What else is there out there? In the far distances where the great fiery planets move along their trackless orbits, making the music of the spheres, what else is there out there except God? And they themselves had got there by laws which they did not create, laws of motion not subject at all to the politburo or to any other parliament. Of course, we can have the notion that we grow beyond God, not only in the sense of our inquiry, or our scientific inquiry, but also in the sense of what we believe to be our status in life. There is an arrogance of place, of race, and yes, of grace, which may lead us to believe that we are beyond the sovereignty of the Eternal. And it is against that kind of notion, the psalmist raises his voice, only to be echoed through all of these succeeding generations and ages: "If I ascend up into heaven, thou art there." And no amount of repudiation of the things of Scripture or claims of loyalty to the Word of God can offset that presence of God in the highest places to which humanity, individually or corporately, may reach.

There was an article in the *Richmond Times Dispatch* yesterday evening which ought to make every American weep and which most assuredly ought to bring a profound lament to the heart of all of those who profess Jesus Christ as Savior and which ought to cut to the quick of those of us who in some sense or another are entrusted with the spiritual welfare of the nation. It was a quotation from the chairwoman of the conference on the Decade of the Woman meeting now in Nairobi. She made the comment, "If things did not go to our liking, while we had no intention of walking out, if things did not go to our liking, they would see what we can do." Do you know what the question, or issue, was to be submitted to their liking? Whether or not Third World people would press a resolution through that conference opposing apartheid in South Africa. How desperately we do need to know that whatever our ascents, however lofty our political altitudes, if we ascend up into heaven, "thou art there." It is something that we all ought to take to heart.

Then there is another word spoken here in this passage: "If I make my bed in hell," if I descend into hell. Ours is an age of, how shall I put it, a compulsive tell-all. It is a kind of era of the *National Enquirer*. People vie in revealing the sleaziest, the most sordid revelation about their family and about themselves. And they do it with a kind of boastfulness; it is in vogue, don't you know, to deal at the edge of filth and violence. There is a sudden stylishness about it, a fashionableness about it. And one can scarcely read today a biography, and surely not an autobiography, without being treated to large portions of this kind of swill. Ours is a time of kiss and tell and sell. It is a characteristic of our generation. I saw a gentleman on a plane who had hidden in the folds of the *New York Daily News* a copy of *Playboy* magazine. I didn't know what he was studying, but he was studying it intensely. Every time someone would come close or the hostess would pass, he would turn to another page. As soon as she passed, he would turn back to his *Playboy,* or *Penthouse,* whatever it was. At any rate, it is characteristic of our time.

You and I run into this kind of insolence; sometimes we may participate in it. We run into it at certain respectable levels, where people say they have little to do with religion, that kind of thing is not their cup of tea. And while they respect the church and all of that, they are not found within its precincts at all. They don't feel the need for it. And our commentator, having delivered himself or herself of that kind of what he or she considers lofty sentiment, looks around as if from alpine heights. I always feel moved, and sometimes I do feel moved to say, "I had a Doberman pinscher once who never exercised any interest in religion either, nor went to church." And sometimes I say to them, if the mood is right, "I know his reason. What is yours?"

The heart of the whole biblical revelation is that God has come; certainly the New Testament asserts that God has come as low as humanity can sink. That is the very meaning of the Incarnation. That he has gotten down in the filth and foulness and vileness of our mortality. That he has condescended to wear as his cloak the corruption of our humanity. That he has made common cause with our weakness, with our limitations, with our incapacities. At Calvary, God in Christ has reached out to the farthest edges of the precipices and got hold of a soul that must have been at home in the brothels of Jerusalem and in the underworld of Galilee and Samaria. At Calvary, God in Christ has said to a criminal, "Today shalt thou be with me in paradise" (Luke 23:43).

The old preachers thought that when that cross upon which our Lord died was struck at the bottom, it not only reached the rock upon that hill, that scarlet hill, but it reached down into the lowest depths of humanity, to the very fires of hell. That was the meaning of that word. When the campfire followers of human experience, thank God for them, the theologians, sat down to codify the faith, they put those words in the Creed describing Christ's downward sweep, saying he "descended into hell," so that the glory of the gospel is that if I make my bed in hell, God is there. There is no violation, there is no transgression, there is no trespass, that lies beyond the compassion of God. Beyond all of our efforts at justice and beyond our lowest depths to which we can fall, the compassion of God still exists.

I wish that I could find a nicer word, but he scoops us up out of degradation. "If I make may bed in hell, behold, thou art there." Also, "if I take the wings of the morning, and dwell in the uttermost parts of the sea" — wings of the morning! Donald Hall, writing in the Sunday *New York Times Magazine,* commented that American speech, once full of vigor and life, has grown feeble and tired. He said that we write so faintly and speak with such passivity that the style we emulate seems to be people who write prescriptions for medicine bottles or government directives. Why this dread of language that reaches out and language that soars? What language the Bible uses! What expanded metaphors! What impossible images! What energy of speech! "The wings of the morning."

What are the wings of the morning? Upon what pinions does the dawn arrive? "The wings of the morning." Stretch your imagination to the farthest reaches of which it is capable. Go out beyond the timberline of the spirit where nothing exists, to the barrenness of spirit, where there is no companionship, no sense of insight. Nothing, loneliness, solitude, the arctic region of the soul. Out there if I take the wings of the morning and flee, God meets me. "Thou art there" — that is the glory of the faith, that there is no circumstance, no condition, in which God is not present.

You and I ought to first believe that in our hearts because of Jesus Christ, and we ought to declare to our people that there are no boundaries beyond which God lacks sovereignty. He does give deliverance to the prisoner in the darkest dungeon. And he does give liberation to the slave in the most dehumanized captivity. That's the heart of the gospel. It is the word that our Lord said to us, in that valedictory assurance set down in the Gospel of Matthew. While a cloud chariot waits to bear him back to his native place, he says to those that gathered around, "Lo, I am with you always, even unto the end of the world. I will be with you, wherever you are. In conditions of bright promise, in times of darkest despair, I will be with you. On the mountain where the sun shines so bright, in the valley in the darkest of night, I will be with you."

There is a hymn greatly loved among that people in whose presence it is my privilege to preach. It says, "I've seen the lightning flash, I've heard the thunder roar, I've felt sin's breakers trying to conquer my soul. I've heard the voice of Jesus telling me still to fight on. He has promised never to leave me alone," nor will he. And now on towards evening, I can confidently say to you that in your ministry and in those places that it has pleased God to call you, or wherever it will please him to call you, he will not forsake you, will not leave you. He'll carry you on, bear you up, and give you a word to speak until your work is finished and the day is over and the evening comes and the shadows fall. He will not leave you, not even then.

∽ 17 ∾

GOD'S PROMISE FOR OUR TEMPTATIONS
1 Corinthians 10:12–13

Wherefore let him that thinketh he standeth take heed lest he fall. There hath no temptation taken you but such as is common to man: but God is faithful, who will not suffer you to be tempted above that ye are able; but will with the temptation also make a way to escape, that ye may be able to bear it. (1 Corinthians 10:12–13)

I have said elsewhere that each of us lives in what may be called a haunted house, built in the region of death. That we live out our days close to death is perhaps too obvious and clear to need any further explanation. But what is meant by saying that we live in a haunted house?

Think of your life as a house, and reflect on how many tenants live in that residence. How many guests, good and bad, polite and impolite, come in and pass out of your experience? What ghosts of memory flit eerily? and what phantom figures out of the past move often unbidden and unbeckoned through our remembrances, flashing before us like pictures on a television screen? I have thought lately of the night and day following our great fire over twenty-five years ago and the people, so many who have passed from sight, who were involved as we started on the long road back toward getting a church building. They happily haunt my reverie.

A haunted house? Yes, our lives are haunted houses. Friendly ghosts, good memories, move to and fro. There are many other guests who visit us, some bidden, others who come without invitation and without welcome. Sorrow and sickness, disappointment and discouragement, misunderstanding and confusion, and a host of other unwelcome guests come to our lives at one time or another.

105

Among them is temptation. The Scriptures doubtlessly intend to lump under that word all that puts faithfulness to God under test. W. H. D. Faunce, president of Brown University many years ago, once lectured to the students of that school in morning chapel on "Temptations Upward." In it he spoke of the aim of the university to tempt, to entice, and to attract students upward toward an appreciation for the noble things of art and learning. Surely there are temptations toward better things: allurements upward.

The Scriptures, however, use the word *temptation* in a different way. Scripturally, temptation usually is that which tests our faithfulness to God. Temptation in the Scriptures suggests something mean, undermining, no friend to help us on to God. Surely this is true of the New Testament, for the first time we meet the word *temptation* it is upon the lips of our Lord, and it represents something to be shunned as he teaches us how we ought to pray: "Lead us not into temptation, but deliver us from evil" (Matthew 6:13).

Every one of us must face times, places, and circumstances that test our faithfulness to God. Anything which tries to pull you away from your loyalty to your God as you have known him in Jesus Christ is a temptation. The apostle Paul reminds us that no one must feel so secure in his or her faith that one feels beyond the power of temptation. No one gets so righteous that temptation does not come.

We read of our Lord being tempted in the wilderness by Satan himself. Three times the evil one subjected Christ to temptation. Jesus faced the temptation of physical welfare: "Hungry, are you? Make bread of these stones just to prove that you are the Son of God." No! Round one was over. Round two: "You want people to follow you? Leap from this high and dizzying pinnacle of the temple, for he, God, your psalmist said, will give his angels charge over you to keep you in all your ways." No! End of round two. Round three: "Look! All of the kingdoms of this world are stretched in breathtaking panorama before you. Fall down and worship me, and I will give all these things unto you." No! Round three was over, and the Lord Jesus would not fall. Luke's account of the temptation then says a surprising thing: "When the devil had ended all the temptation, he departed from him for a season" (4:13). Now, if Jesus our Lord had to face temptations, then surely we who claim our place among his friends and disciples must realize that we will face temptation. Nobody is exempt. "Wherefore, let him that thinketh he standeth, take heed lest he fall."

The powers of evil, be they impersonal principles or evil spirits, demons, powers loose in the world, reach at God's best people. The evil forces are out to embarrass the Kingdom and to throw shame on God's name and the honor of Jesus Christ. They tempt us to turn on each other and to seek to hurt each other in the household of faith. I have seen it. As soon as a man's spiritual influence grows strong and as soon as a woman's power in service to God enlarges, the powers of hell go to work. Envy, misunderstanding, wicked gossip, and a tissue of lies and half-truths begin to appear.

Now, it is a fair game I suppose for the enemies of the cross to seek to weaken the influence of God's people, but it is an abomination for those who call themselves the Lord's people to join forces with hell in trying to destroy the influence of a single soul the Lord is using. If and when you join in damaging a brother's reputation or a sister's good name in the household of faith, you are an ally of hell; you enter an alliance with evil. I name you now, you talebearers, you gossipmongers, you slander merchants — partners of hell, enemies of God — these are your titles. Let me pass from this consideration with the solemn words of Jesus our Lord. "It is impossible," said Jesus, "but that offenses will come; but woe unto him, through whom they come! It were better for him that a millstone were hanged about his neck, and he cast into the sea, than that he should offend one of these little ones" (Luke 17:1–2).

We must expect that temptation, all kinds, will come upon us. Nor will they ever stop, for the devil left our Lord only for a season. Of course as the song says, "Each victory will help us some other to win," but temptations will come. The masks that temptation wears are of endless variety. The temptation of spiritual weariness, the temptation of pride, the temptation of spiritual laziness, the temptation of spitefulness, the temptation of envy, the temptation of greed, the temptation to lie, the temptation of lust, and the temptation of stinginess and thanklessness toward God! My Father, the temptations are without number!

The Lord advises us through the apostle Paul to look upon temptations with due seriousness but not in terror or fear. These enemies who seem so grim, so terrible, so invincible, who seem to have picked us out for their special attack, have been met by the saints of the Lord. They are old characters, and God and his people know them. Their number has been taken, and their force has been met by others. I think as we get older and are called on to face this and that, we see more clearly what our fathers and mothers and our other elders went through. They told us we would too, saying, "Keep on living." Yes, and something more, as we face one thing and then another, we remember how they, in God, met and matched, confronted and conquered, all that life could do, even unto death. Thank God, the perilous temptations and the tempting troubles which storm at us are those that are common to God's people. And in that remembering we take hope. What men and women have done, in God we can do.

Nor does the promise end there: "God is faithful, who will not suffer you to be tempted above that ye are able" (1 Corinthians 10:13). How often we feel that we just cannot stand another sorrow or another disappointment. How often we feel we have already borne all we can stand. We believe that we have taken all we can, but God knows, actually knows, how much we can bear. God has a stake in what happens to us. God's honor and God's reputation are involved in what happens to his people who acknowledge him as God and Father. Do you think for a moment God would stand by and see his children beaten down and not step in? He loves and cherishes every movement of a soul toward him, toward godliness, toward holiness unto him, and he will not stand by and let us lose the battle. God is faithful! Say it to yourself when all hell rises against you. God is faithful! Repeat it when the hellhounds are baying on your trail, all earthly help has failed, and friends have walked away. God is faithful! Remember it when dark clouds gather and strong winds blow. Whisper it in sickness and in sorrow. God is faithful! Let all oppressed people everywhere know that the strength of the Almighty belongs to those of "low estate."

"[He] will with the temptation also make a way to escape." Now God's deliverances do not come before the moment of need. That would be poor divine drama. God moves in the nick of time, in the fullness of time, and when all things are ready. God gave Abraham a ram in the thicket only when his hand was upraised to slay his little child, Isaac. God opened the Red Sea only when the chariot wheels of Pharaoh's army thundered in the ears of a trembling Israel. God raised up Joshua to lead only when Moses fell on death's sleep in the hills of Mount Nebo.

With the temptation, there comes a way out. God hides the way out inside the temptation. God puts daybreak in the midnight. God puts peace in the confusion. God puts healing in the hurt. It is as if he says to whatever or whoever it is that stands against his child, "You strike, and I will protect. You hurt, and I will heal. You slander, and I will glorify. You embarrass, and I will honor. You pull down, and I will lift up. You curse, and I will bless. You block the path; I will open a highway. You close the door, and I will open it. You muddy my child, and I will clean him until he stands in the spotlessness of my own righteousness."

So in it all, God makes us able to praise him, to thank him, to love him, to honor him, to serve him, to enjoy him, to trust him, and to follow him.

∞ 18 ∞

A Great New Testament "I Am"

John 10:9

> I am the door: by me if any man enter in, he shall be saved, and shall go in and out, and find pasture. (John 10:9)

In an earlier year I attempted to preach a series of sermons on what I called some "I AM" sayings of Jesus. One who reads the words of the Savior cannot help being struck by the self-assured way in which Jesus spoke of himself, though the most lofty references our Lord made to himself seem to be neither exaggeration nor conceit. What on any other man's lips would sound like the sickeningly egotistical rantings of a self-centered madman, a megalomaniac, seems perfectly natural when Jesus says it.

In John's Gospel, Jesus says, "I am the door." He was talking about access to life. It will not be many more sentences in this wonderful series of sayings before our Lord states bluntly and clearly the whole purpose and point of his ministry and life, "I am come that they might have life, and that they might have it more abundantly" (v. 10). So when Jesus said, "I am the door," he was talking about being the opening, the passageway, the entranceway to life because he is the way to God. "I am the door," not, mind you, "I know the location to the door that leads to life." That would send us thrilling and vibrating to find someone who knows where the opening into life and God may be found. Jesus' word is far stronger, "I am the door."

In this lovely word picture "I am the door," Jesus was referring to how the sheep of Palestine were kept out on the hillsides in the warm part of the year. During such a season, the sheepfolds were enclosures, large pens, so to speak, surrounded by improvised walls or barriers. There would be an opening in the enclosure about the length of a human body. At night, when the

110

danger of wild animals and sheep thieves became a pressing problem, the sheep would be brought into the enclosure with the one opening, and the shepherd would lie across the opening to keep and protect the sheep. Thus no enemy could get in or out without crossing the stretched-out body of the shepherd.

It was to this simple and familiar scene Jesus referred when he said, "I am the door." Jesus is for us Christians the means by which we get to God. The old preachers spoke of him as our "go-between," but the figure here is of a door, a means of entrance. Through him, men and women find an avenue, an entrance to God and, therefore, to life itself. In Ephesians 2:18, the inspired writer told us, "Through him," meaning Jesus, "we have access...unto the Father," and the writer of Hebrews let us know that "Christ is the new and living way." Christ then for us is the door to God.

It is sometimes in our ordinary dealing a matter of life or death to know the location of a door. We read now and then of terrible tragedies in which great numbers of people are trampled to death in some public building in the midst of a fire, or in sudden darkness, because people in the crowded place could not find the door. It can also be a great privilege to be able to go through a door, even when one knows the location. How many of us have had to stand looking at doors beyond which were the things we needed, yet we were denied the right to go through the door? Some may not go through the door of registering and voting, but I could tell you of fearful and dangerous times when people risked their lives to try to get that door opened for black people. Some I knew died in the effort.

There are doors where for one reason or another we cannot enter because we are outsiders. I remember well a preaching engagement some years ago in the stately city of Adelaide in South Australia. Staying at the Grosvenor Hotel, I would walk over each evening to the Flinders Street Baptist Church, where the services were held. The passing of nearly twenty years has not erased from memory a particular evening of homesickness at being ten thousand miles from home and family, which came over me like a physical ache. The time of evening was that strangely touching hour when day turns quietly to night and all of the family have come from here and there to gather in the light and warmth and joy of home. I looked at such a house, a lamp burning in what I took to be the living room with the family gathered there. It was not my family nor my home, and the door was closed to me. I thought of home and kin, and a sickness almost physical settled for a moment over me as I walked on through the cool evening darkness to the church.

Thank God, Jesus says that the fold, the gathering for which he is the entranceway, is open to one and all. There is no test of eligibility. Though it has not always been followed, one of the cardinal principles of the American political system is that there shall be no religious test for holding office in this country. The invitation of Jesus is far wider than that. It opens to whosoever will: "I am the door: by me if any man enter in, he shall be saved, and shall go in and out, and find pasture." This door which is Christ is open for all: the sinner is invited to enter; the thief may come; the adulterer is not shut out; the murderer may go in; the liar can be admitted; the drunkard need have no fear if he desires to enter there. The drug addict is not excluded, and the gambler is not prevented. All that one needs is a desire, a will, to enter there. I am so glad for that word *any*. It is my invitation signed by Jesus. It is my admittance card bearing Calvary's seal. It is my reservation ticket with the blood marks of Jesus upon it. Any man! Any woman!

"He shall be saved." Now, there is a large and theological meaning to this word *saved*. In those places where faith matters are closely and systematically studied, what is usually meant by the word *saved* is gathered up under the technical subject of soteriology. It includes the doctrines of the fall of humanity from the state of innocence in Eden, the consequence of sin, the redemptive work of Christ, and the redeemed soul's eternal destiny. Soteriology is a great and wonderful consideration, but here our Lord is, I think, speaking of something far simpler, far more local, bearing a much greater immediacy. Dr. J. B. Phillips has, I believe, translated this word *saved* here most exactly and accurately as "safe and sound." Then we might read, "I am the door. If any many goes in through me, he will be safe and sound."

One cannot say too often that such safety in Jesus does not mean exemption from any life experience. It means rather "safe in," not "safe from," whatever may happen. And much may happen. We have only to think a moment. Life is filled with dangers and barren places, and a great solitude in spite of love and companionship. Life is a long, dusty march, and there are lurking foes, grim rocks, fierce heat, parched wells, and burned-out sandy wastes. Who knows what our eyes will meet when we top the next hill or round the next curve in this perilous journey? Does some lurking terror even now wait to pounce out on you or me like some dread and hungry beast? In it and through it, all of us are safe if we are of the fold of Jesus Christ.

I would stress once again that we are not spared troubles and trials, but we are protected and preserved in the midst of them. There are hothouse plants which blossom well in unvarying temperatures, but they lack something heroic which one sees in a great oak tree or on a wild rose bush that in heat and cold, in storm and sun, continues to live and grow. So we are "safe" not from but in our troubles. There are children who cannot play as ordinary children, for they have a disease called "hemophilia," the tendency to bleed profusely and to hemorrhage from the slightest skin break. One of the royal houses of Europe suffered from that. Children who suffer with hemophilia cannot play rough children's games; they must be protected from anything which might produce a scar or a cut. On the other hand, a child who is to be a normal adult must get scratches and cuts. It is a part of growing up. So we are "safe" through Christ in our troubles and trials. He does not prevent me from having enemies; "he prepares a table before me in the presence of my enemies."

"I am the door. If a man goes in through me, he will be safe and sound; he can come in and out and find his food" (Phillips). The Old Testament speaks in Numbers 27:17 of going out and coming in in connection with the leader of a people who "may go out before them, and which may go in before them, and which may lead them out, and which may bring them in; that the congregation of the Lord be not as sheep which have no shepherd." Again in Deuteronomy, the benediction of conditionality is made upon Israel: "If thou shalt hearken diligently unto the voice of the LORD thy God, . . . Blessed shalt thou be when thou comest in, and blessed shalt thou be when thou goest out" (28:1,6). That lovely Psalm 121 says, "The LORD shall preserve thy going out and thy coming in from this time forth, and even for evermore" (v. 8).

So here we are told that Christ is the door, and if we come in by him, we shall be saved, and we shall go in and out and find pasture. Thus we are assured the rhythm of the blessed life in God. We may go out to serve the world and to exercise our strength, but we must first get that strength. We may go out to apply our gifts and to do our work in the world, but we first need to receive energy and power. The world needs help. It needs guidance. People need those who can make the load a little lighter. So we must go out. But, heaven knows, before we go out, we need to go in and get help from the Lord.

Christ is the door by which we may go in where God is, may go into the depths of the divine love, and may go in where we may dwell a little while in "the secret place of the most High" (Psalm 91:1). It is through Christ that we may go in where we may walk among the golden candlesticks and behold the inmost shrine of the temple or prayer and worship. Christ lets us in where we may learn "to comprehend with all saints what is the breadth, and the length, and depth, and height" of the full scope of the divine purpose, the redemptive work of God in all of its vast dimensions and eternal meanings (Ephesians 3:18). Passing by way of Christ Jesus, we may enter into the *sanctum sanctorum*, the Holy of Holies, where God feeds his people with manna from on high and leads them to the healing waters and the everlasting fountains and shows them visions older than the world and newer than tomorrow. "In and out" where Christ leads us, our souls are fed, our strength is renewed, our joy is made full, our peace is secured, our calling and election are made sure, and the Holy Spirit leads us into all truth.

I spoke at the beginning about a great second Testament "I AM." That implies that there is a first Testament "I AM." There is! When he was told to go back to Egypt to free the slaves, Moses said to God that the people would ask him who sent him, saying, "What is his name? what shall I say unto them? And God said unto Moses, I AM THAT I AM" (Exodus 3:13–14). So Moses went saying, "The great I AM hath sent me" — not "was" or "will be" but "am," everlastingly now.

Here in the New Testament Jesus by many emblems speaks of his divine sonship and his royal lordship in what I call the great "I AM" words of Jesus. Listen to him: "I am the bread of life" (John 6:35), "I am the light of the world" (John 8:12), "I am Alpha and Omega" (Revelation 1:11), and here, "I am the door." Christ then is the New Testament "I AM." Thus Christ is now and will forever be a sure door to God, a safe door, a wide door, a door of hope, a door of joy, a door to life, a door to heaven, a door to eternity, an open door, the only door. Make Jesus your all, and you will find in him all you need. He is a great Savior, a blessed door, always our Way to God. Entering by him, you may tell the world where e'er you go, you've found the Savior.

∽ 19 ⌣

His Own Clothes

Mark 15:20

And when they had mocked him, they took off the purple from him, and put his own clothes on him, and led him out to crucify him. (Mark 15:20)

Short of the cross itself and the betrayal by Judas, what the soldiers did to Jesus may well have been the most humiliating part of our Lord's suffering and death for you and me. We may be greatly wronged and deeply hurt, but we want to be able to hold on to our human dignity, the feeling that we are a part of the family of humankind. Great suffering may be visited upon us, but there can be a certain nobility, a mark of grandeur, in the way people hold their heads high and bear bravely whatever it is they must go through.

There is something uniquely cruel in being laughed at and mocked, set apart from one's fellows and made the target of ugly jibes, cruel comment, and cutting laughter. One of the most painful and sinister weapons used historically against black people in this country was mockery and ridicule. Physical features were caricatured and exaggerated, and so the large white-lipped, wide-eyed, blackened faces in minstrel shows became the notion of the way black people looked and acted. I am not far enough from the experience of that mockery to be able to see the art in this kind of thing, no matter what the occasion may be. The purpose of the foot-shuffling, head-scratching, wide-grinning, ghost-frightened darky was to ridicule, scorn, and humiliate. Every southern town once had its village idiot whom children would shamefully taunt. Children who are different know how cruel such horseplay can be.

Far crueler than our own experience was the kind of scorn and

ridicule that the soldiers heaped upon our Lord on the night leading to his crucifixion. While it may be true that the sport these
members of the praetorian guard, Pilate's military escort, made of
Jesus had little venom in it, still it chills the spirit to think of the
Son of God, the Savior of the world, the blessed Redeemer, being the object of the rude jokes and the broad barracks' humor of
these rough and dull-witted soldiers.

The Master moved toward his death on our behalf over a road
that grew constantly more steep and more terrifying. First, there
was his inner agony in Gethsemane. This was followed by betrayal, after which the chains were put on Jesus as a common
criminal. Later that night they blindfolded our Lord and then
struck him a stinging slap in the face taunting, "Prophesy. Who
is it that smote thee?" Then they did spit in his face to add to the
outrage. Each new assault seemed designed to outdo the last.

Following all of these things, they scourged the Lord. This
painful humiliation probably took place on the platform where
the trial had been held and in sight of all. The victim was stripped
down to the waist and was stretched against a pillar with hands
tied. The instrument of torture was a long leather strip, studded
with pieces of lead and bits of bone. The whip left lashes, and the
lead and bone tore out chunks of flesh. Some died under the lash,
and others emerged from the torture raving mad. Through all of
these things Jesus passed in the interest of all of our souls. All of
these things, as horrible and as appalling as they are, were but
preliminary and secondary to the supreme sacrifice of Calvary. So
we read that after the Lord was scourged with the lash, sentence
was pronounced, and it was the sentence of death by crucifixion,
the most awful and painful of the Roman methods of execution.
Cicero declared that it was "the most cruel and horrifying death."
(William Barclay thought that the Romans picked up this method
of execution from the Persians, who believed the earth was sacred and wished to avoid defiling it with an evildoer.) Lifted on
a cross, the condemned slowly died, and the vultures and carrion
crows might dispose of the body.

The Roman ritual of condemnation and execution was fixed.

Sentence was pronounced, "Let him be crucified." The sentence was that this man should be hung on the cross. Then the judge turned to the guard and said, "Go, soldier, and prepare the cross." It was at this point that Jesus our Lord was turned over to the soldiers who formed the personal guard of Pilate as governor.

These men were hard-bitten professional soldiers who chafed at their unpleasant assignment in such a hot, fly-ridden place as Palestine and among all of those strange and offensive people. They took their pastime and sport when and where they could find them. One of their pleasures was to taunt and torture convicted criminals who cringed before them like cornered and helpless animals. The Son of God was turned over to them, and they went to work with their cruel jibes.

The whole detachment gathered in their barracks with the Savior of the world before them and, as they thought, in their hands. They stripped him of his clothes. Having picked up some thread of the charge that Jesus claimed to be a king, they jammed a reed in his hand to mock a scepter, plaited a crown made out of thorn bush for his brow, and flung around the Lord's shoulder an old, faded red tunic, the scarlet cloak that was a part of the parade uniform of the Roman soldier. All this was done to mock him as a king, and so they bowed down in ridicule as if to honor and worship him. "We will be your devotees and subjects, King Jesus. Look at us kneeling before you," and then their loud, uncouth laughter rang and echoed through the barracks.

There are still many who put cloaks of imitation honor and false respect on the Lord Jesus as surely as those soldiers put their old scarlet robe on the Savior. Such do not mean their patronizing words of respect about the Lord Jesus. You can hear them now and again. One says, "I respect and honor Jesus. His golden rule is enough religion for anybody to live by. I admire his life and believe it to be a thing of beauty. His ethics are splendid principles of conduct and human relations."

As for his church and all of that, these smart people are very lofty: "It is all right for those who need it, but I do not go to church. I do not feel the need of it, really." And so saying, they feel they have delivered themselves of something very profound and, if not profound, then chic and fashionable. Well, I had a dog, a blooded Doberman pinscher, who never went to church either. I feel like answering such glib dismissal of the church for which Christ died by saying, "My dog did not go to church either. He never felt the need of it because he was a dog. Now, what is your reason?"

There are still others who put garments of mock royalty on the Lord and who call his name but who feel no deep loyalty to him, no crowning and controlling love for the Lord, who has done so much for us. You may see them now and again in church, now and then among the people of Christ. They throw their leftovers at the Lord who made us all, as one would toss scraps to a pet dog. They are neither hot nor cold, and to such the word of the Revelation applies, "I will spew thee out of my mouth" (3:16).

There is a lot of sham religion in this country, people going through the motions for whom Christ is not a living, determining presence. Again and again people ask, "What is wrong with us as a nation?" One word is the answer: godlessness. Never mind the churches and synagogues and mosques; godlessness is what is wrong with us. Never mind the public prayers and taking oaths on the Bible. Godlessness is what is wrong with America. How does it come out? In the swagger of a gun lobby and money that stops congressmen from passing a gun law. In greed and bigotry and the attitude "anything goes." In lies and deceit in a nation that has no room for worship or things of the spirit.

You ask what is wrong with us as a people. Listen to any national telecast. See how all of our national interest is built around what some self-serving people in Washington do: crime, scams, confusion. See how little of the heart and mind, how little room for things of the spirit, there is in our national telecasts. Godlessness! And until we turn to the Lord, it will not get better; it will get worse. And, yes, one thing after another will go wrong.

Have I put fake garments on the Lord Jesus? Have I cloaked the Savior of the world in scarlet robes of pretense, claiming that I honor him as Lord while my heart is far from him? Do I take my faith in the Lord Jesus seriously? Am I willing, as George Eliot put it, to sacrifice anything for him as long as the result is not unpleasant?

And then we read that when the soldiers had tired of their ugly game of ridicule and making sport of the Son of God, they took off the old scarlet tunic and put his own clothes back on him. This was the final preparation for crucifixion. They put on our Lord his own clothes. And "his own clothes" says worlds to us. We need to see him as he is, "in his own clothes," not mocked and ridiculed by false respect and pious hypocrisy. When we see the Lord "in his own clothes," in his true character and force, we see someone who makes us cry out for forgiveness and for his good favor and approval. Looking at Jesus as he is, we see ourselves as we are.

When our Christ is not mocked by false garments of respectable sneer or false enthusiasm, when we see him in his own clothes as he is, we want to do better. Dr. Donald Shelby, the California United Methodist preacher, has told of a terrible storm on Lake Michigan in which a ship was wrecked near the shore. A Northwestern University student, Edmond Spenser, went into the raging water again and again and single-handedly rescued seventeen people. When friends carried him to his room, nearly exhausted and faint, he kept asking them, "Did I do my best?" In the presence of Christ we ask, "Lord, did I do my best?" I am a preacher, and each time I preach I must ask, "Lord, did I do my best?" Officer, choir member, usher, did you do your best?

Jesus in his own clothes going to Calvary did his best. His garments on that lonely hill were rolled in blood, making understandable the old cry of Isaiah, "Who is this that cometh from Edom, with dyed garments from Bozrah? this that is glorious in his apparel, travelling in the greatness of his strength? (Isaiah 63:1). We ask, "Wherefore art thou red in thine apparel, and thy garments [thy clothes] like him that treadeth in the winevat?" (v. 2). And he answers, "I have trodden the winepress alone.... For the day of vengeance is in mine heart, and the year of my redeemed is come" (vv. 3–4).

In his own clothes he went to Calvary and made everything all right, not temporarily all right but for always. At Calvary Christ was at his best. Nothing had been left undone. On no other day does Jesus have to go back to finish his work at Calvary. This he did once. "Now once in the end of the world hath he appeared to put away sin by the sacrifice of himself.... So Christ was once offered to bear the sins of many" (see Hebrews 9:26–28). He died in his own clothes as Savior and Redeemer. Once for all. It is all right now. The crooked way has been made straight; we may arise and shine for light is come. It is all right now.

We shall see him yet in other clothes. Ellen White, the prophetess of Seventh-Day Adventism, pictures that day when Christ shall appear no longer with an old, faded red cloak around his shoulders, no longer mocked by soldiers, no longer wearing simple garments of this earth. Every eye shall see him. We will see him as heaven's King, victor over death, hell, and the grave, the admired of angels. Every eye shall see him. Ten thousand times ten thousand and thousands and thousands of angels and the triumphant sons and daughters of God will escort him. His raiment will outshine the sun. And on his vesture, his clothes, a name will be written, "King of kings and Lord of lords." Shall we not shout his name who has lifted us to heights sublime and made us his own people forever?

ᵔ 20 ᵔ

How Not to Faint

Luke 18:1

And he spake a parable unto them to this end, that men ought always to pray, and not to faint. (Luke 18:1)

I greet all of you on this Memorial Day weekend and congratulate you on what has not yet come to pass. You cannot know now how well off you are. You will know tomorrow evening when the people who struggled to leave the city spend all of whatever enjoyment they got leaving trying to get back. Some years ago, I found myself having to oppose a theory which was being advanced as to what our black preaching and worshiping had been in the generations that are gone. My impression was that some people were, in utter sincerity I am sure, advancing the idea that our whole black religious enterprise in this country, I refer particularly to our preaching and our participation in worship, has been a kind of half-comic entertainment, filled with defective language, broken grammar, and dialect. Now to be sure, there was, as there is now, some brokenness in our grammar and in our language, but I heard the preachers of fifty years ago, and I witnessed the worship of our people in those years long gone. And there was a loftiness to the language, a grandeur in their phrases which I found most appealing, and still do.

Many years ago now, I had the privilege of preaching an anniversary service for the oldest black Baptist church in America. I know it was the oldest in Savannah, from which some of you perhaps come. The First African Baptist Church and the Bryan First African Baptist Church both claim to be the oldest existing black Baptist church in America. That year during the ministries of Ralph Mark Gilbert and Richard Williams, both of whom now are in the Father's House, the two churches came together for

122

their anniversary service. And so it was guaranteed, whichever was the first, in that occasion the anniversary of the oldest black Baptist church was being observed. After the service there was a pilgrimage out to a cemetery which went back to the 1700s. I remember vividly the moss in the trees and our standing at an old tomb somewhat in decay. It was the tomb of the founder of the First African Baptist Church of Savannah. And in the inscription on the tomb, I'm sure written by some black person, there was the line that that founder, and I quote now, "had been made meet," had been made ready, "for Emmanuel's bosom." What a magnificent phrase, going back to the early 1800s. And when one heard the prayers of early blacks which James Weldon and his brother James Rosemond Johnson made literary gems, what lofty language meets us, what classic language was in one of our prayers. It went, "We come," and I remember hearing it, "knee bent and body bowed. Our hearts below our knees, and our knees in some lonesome valley." Or that other word, "We come as empty pitchers before a full fountain." Grand language.

Among those gentlefolks who were my elders, we had on Thursday night before every first Sunday what was called "Speaking Meeting." People told their, what we call, "determination," "testimony"; people gave their testimony. I remember now the lines of my elders, God bless their memories, "I come before you one more time in life to tell you my determination. My determination is for heaven and immortal glory. I ask your prayers that my last days will be my best and heaven will be my home." "My last days my best" — it was their plea, their prayer, that they might not come to an end and quit, give up, let down, turn back. "That my last days be my best." I would think the greatest peril for Christian people is the peril of quitting along this way, fainting, for the Bible speaks again and again of fainting. Not schoolgirl swooning, but fainting in the sense of losing heart, of coming at last to a dim view of things, of weakening, of collapsing, of failing, of turning back. I would guess it could be safely argued that the apostle Paul was easily ranked among the greatest Christians these twenty centuries have seen. He speaks himself of the danger, of an awful and chilling fear he had. "That lest," he said, "when I preached the gospel to others, I myself might become a castaway." Unapproved! And everybody in Christian service might ponder that, rejected, unapproved.

What is it that makes us faint, give up? How sad it is to see somebody who starts off in a great blaze of enthusiasm, and then somewhere along the way a chill sets in. How sad to see a young man or a young woman start in life's work, their life's work, with a zeal and a blazing determination to give a good account of themselves, and then somewhere along the line, that determination withers. And there at last there they are sort of meandering, staggering along in some kind of fashion. What is it that makes us faint, that makes us give up, lose heart, turn back, quit?

Well, life's experiences are tough. Sometimes they are almost too tough for any of us. Many people find out that the way is not as simple as it seems. We are in commencement season now. There was a time when they would put those fine, brave mottoes up over the stage in the little schools: "Excelsior" and "Forever onward and upward." But we discover in the experiences of life that it does not just go forever onward and upward. This life is an uneven journey. We're sometimes up, and we're sometimes down! There are things, great trials, that test our very souls. And we're likely to faint. And sometimes it is not one big thing, but just a congregation, a gathering of a lot of little things. The book of Canticles, which did not make the Bible, has a passage in it about the little foxes that destroy the fields. Sometimes things just mount up as a multiplication of problems until they, one little one after the other, pile up, our patience runs out, and we feel that there's no point in it. And sometimes we faint, we give up, because our family and our friends place demands upon us that we are unable to meet. Added to that is our own burden of guilt, the sins that drain our spiritual energy and leave us spent and exhausted.

Friends do not prove true sometimes; we do not prove true to them. I suppose it is true to say that often friends, our friends, do us more harm than our enemies, often very innocently, not intending at all. But all these things come together, and we discover that we're not equal. And so we hardly have a choice...well we do have a choice, but we find a false solution to the whole thing: to quit, give up! It's not turning out right. The collapse of our black family in America has been attributed often and partly, I think, truthfully to that. Our menfolk, our males, facing the awful odds of this society just do not feel equal to carrying the load. And not measuring up, they give up.

What do we do? Well, Jesus puts it to us clearly here in the beginning of the eighteenth chapter of the Gospel of Luke. He says, "Men ought always to pray, and not to faint." What is he saying to us? He is saying, is he not, that praying and fainting cannot live under the same roof, that one must go, that when we truly pray, energy is given to us so that we do not have to faint. "Men ought always to pray," he said. Pray whenever whatever happens. Pray always, always. Not sometimes, but pray always. If Jesus is our example, then we have a mighty lesson in prayer because he prayed in bright days and in dark nights. He prayed his way through life and through death and into victory. That day at the Jordan River, Luke tells us, when he was to be baptized, he prayed in an initial act of consecration, prayed until the heavens opened. And God spoke from on high and said, "This is my beloved Son, in whom I am well pleased."

He prayed all night long the night before he chose his disciples, because our judgment is blind, except in God's light. Our wisdom is too meager, except the Lord guide our direction and our decision. He prayed all night before he chose his disciples. And at the mount of transfiguration he prayed until the borderline between heaven and earth disappeared. Prayed until time edged momentarily into eternity. He prayed until Moses heard him and Elijah answered. They came and stood there on that bright mountain with him; he prayed until heaven came down. In Gethsemane in the fourth watch of the night, his own fourth watch, he prayed alone until angels came down and wiped the sweat from his brow. He prayed! On Calvary in the midst of the agony and pain, he prayed until the debt was settled for the murderers who were murdering him. Prayed until the account was settled. Prayed until they were forgiven. Prayed until death lost its sting. Prayed until heaven sang again. And finally, he prayed his own spirit into the Father's hands. He prayed the surrender of his spirit into the keeping of the Father: "Into thy hands I commend my spirit." Jesus prayed when things went well, and prayed when things went against him. Prayed when friends were all around him, and prayed when he had no friends. Prayed by day, prayed by night, prayed in the temple, and prayed alone, prayed his way through life and beyond.

And you and I ought to pray. Pray on, my brother and my sister. Pray on when success smiles on your pathway. Pray lest life turn your head away from God. When failure clouds your day, pray because God will bring you sunshine. Pray when life turns mean, for in prayer's sweet hour, the soul has often found relief and oft escaped the tempter's snare. Pray on. Pray on in sickness, for God can cool the scorching fever. Pray on when sorrow comes, for God can wipe all tears from your eyes. Pray on when trouble comes to your house; pray until it has to run away. Pray when friends forsake you, because Jesus is a friend that sticks closer than a brother; pray on. Pray when your way is dark and lonely, for he will cheer the weary traveler; pray on.

Someone says, "Is it not easy?" And I answer back, "It is not." There are times when it is almost impossible, and it is impossible for us to pray unaided. If we are alone calling on God, even on our own behalf, by ourselves, then we may not be able. . . . Sickness can be so deep, sorrow can be so complete, anger can be so much in control, that our prayers seem not to rise above the roof of the house. We can pray if we are companioned, but sometimes we cannot count on that on earth. I have said to you that when my mother lived, I always felt confident, whether I was on land or sea or in the air or under whatever circumstance, that she was praying for me. Sometimes now, I do not know. Still, every child of God prays with aid all around. Maybe somebody here in the world is praying for you! I hope so. But if nobody, hear me carefully, on earth is praying for you, your prayer is not by itself.

The first chapter of the book of Hebrews says that when Jesus, our Great High Priest, all "by himself purged our sins," with nobody to help him. When Jesus by himself had purged our sins, he sat down on the right hand of the Majesty on high and sat down at God's right hand. What is he doing there? What is he doing there? What's he doing at the right hand of Majesty? What is his occupation? What is his vocation? What does he do? The book of Hebrews in the seventh chapter says, "He ever liveth to make intercession for us." So when the storms of life are raging, my soul cries out. He sits at the right hand of Majesty. Sometimes I think he leans over and says, "Still the storm for him." Ah, when strength runs out, Jesus, sitting there at the right hand of the Majesty on high, I think, leans over and says, "Give him a little more grace." While I am praying and you are praying, he is praying for us, right there at God's right hand, talking to the Father on our behalf, asking him that the dark clouds might be beaten back. Asking him!

And when I and you come down to the Jordan...I think about that now more and more; it is only natural. I cannot tell how it will be, and you cannot tell how it will be. But if you are the Lord's, if you belong to him, I believe when you call, he will answer with all you need....You know, the Scriptures say that once he wasn't sitting there, for when Deacon Stephen got stoned, Christ stood up. I believe when we come down to the river which has no bridge and hear old Jordan pounding in our ears and feel that spray misting our faces, I believe he will hear our cry and carry us over to where the wicked cease from troubling and weary souls are at rest.

∽ 21 ∾

A Human Request and a Divine Reply

John 14:8–9

Philip saith unto him, Lord, show us the Father, and it sufficeth us. Jesus saith unto him, Have I been so long time with you, and yet hast thou not known me, Philip? he that hath seen me hath seen the Father; and how sayest thou then, Show us the Father? (John 14:8–9)

Somewhere that most searching preacher Carlyle Marney spoke of our "essential anxiety" which comes of having to live life making decisions that are not clear-cut and often having to look back upon them and wonder if we made the right choice. In our human contract, this is one of the most burdensome of stipulations.

There is one other item in our human contract which has an even greater importance and upon which our existence turns yet more critically. It is the question, the issue, the consideration, look upon it as you will, as to whether we human beings are in this whole business of living by ourselves. Is there anybody here except us "chickens," so to speak? Sometimes we call out or cry out or scream out for help. Is what we hear, or think we hear, only the echo of our own cry coming back at us from out of an endless emptiness? We speak of Another, a Supreme Being, a Father wonderfully kind, but is that kind of talk only the projection of our own desires, wish fulfillment, a piteous make-believe created because we are afraid to be alone here in this great and frightening world? We wonder sometimes if we are orphans with no one who watches over us and no one who cares about us. This is the pivotal question. In other words, is there a God anywhere? And if so, what is he like? Is he? And if he is, can we relate to him? Can we trust him, her, or however you wish to speak of God?

This is what troubled Philip while Jesus spoke the tenderest words ever uttered on earth about the sadness built into life and love, of that frightening shadow of death which hangs over our own lives and which threatens all of our true love affairs and all of our family joy. The words which almost everyone can repeat were spoken in what is now the beginning of the fourteenth chapter of the Gospel of John. Some of us cannot repeat those words without a catch in the throat, the mist of a tear in the eye, and a bit of a stab in the heart, rendered here partly as Dr. Edgar J. Goodspeed translated them in *The Short Bible.*

> Your minds must not be troubled; you must believe in God, and believe in me. There are many rooms in my Father's house; if there were not, I would have told you, for I am going away to make ready a place for you. And if I go and make it ready, I will come back and take you with me, so that you may be where I am. You know the way. (John 14:1–4)

Were words ever spoken on earth as tender and as comforting as these?

It is interesting to notice that twice in the course of this supremely important discourse, Jesus was interrupted, and twice he showed an almost astonishingly gentle manner in dealing with the interruptions. How annoying it is when we are engaged with great and mighty matters to have someone break in with some trivial, picayune chatter that has about it neither rhyme nor reason. We are likely to feel like shouting out, "For God's sake, keep quiet and listen." Not Jesus. Twice, with only the hint of a rebuke, he paused in his momentous peep into eternity.

The first time occurs as Jesus said, "And whither I go ye know, and the way ye know" (v. 4). Thomas, "who always liked the feel of solid ground beneath his feet, and who perhaps had not much poetry in his nature," as Arthur Gossip put it, blurted out, "Wait a minute! No sir, we do not know where you are going, and we do not know the way." Calmly and with quiet patience, Jesus answered, "I am the way, the truth, and the life" (v. 6).

No sooner was Jesus back on his way, telling the little circle that they could look to him and see the divine heartbeat, before Philip injected another interruption. Philip's request formed a part of the basis of this sermon. He wanted things to be made clearer to him: "Lord, show us the Father, and it sufficeth" (v. 8) — and we shall be satisfied.

Now the name *Philip* is Greek, and it may be that contact with the Greek mentality with its penchant for getting to the bottom of things and finding out the essential truth in whatever was being viewed or probed had affected, or infected, Philip's mind. So when Jesus said that people knowing him should know the Father also, Philip thought the time had come to straighten out a matter which had bothered him for a long time. Was Jesus saying that he pointed to God in his teaching? Was he saying that he, Jesus, somehow symbolized God? To Philip it was all too important a matter to be left in limbo, vague, murky, not clear. So Philip cried out, blurted forth, put to Jesus as natural a human request as human lips can ever utter, "Lord, show us the Father, and we shall be satisfied" (RSV).

We must admit that Philip's request is clearly akin to a desire which we have deep in our hearts. We want to know if there is anybody out yonder anywhere who's got the whole world in his hands. Or is this great ball we call "earth" swimming aimlessly and pointlessly in a vast ocean of space? We long to know if there is a God anywhere. We yearn for somebody to hear us when we call and to watch over us while we slumber and sleep and to direct our footsteps. I think we poor mortals could bear anything if we only knew we were not alone.

I join my heart and voice to Philip's: "Lord, show us the Father." We want to know in the long way we must travel alone if there is one who will guide our steps aright. When we have been bruised by life and our hearts are sore and bleeding, we need to know that God will bind up our wounds and drive away our fears. When we are frightened and shivering with terror, we need a Father to put his hand on our spirits and tell them, "Peace, be still" (Mark 4:39). Put me down alongside Philip: "Lord, show us the Father." Show me him who weighed the mountains in scales and the hills in balances; show me him who is our Shepherd and who takes care of all our needs, who leads us beside still waters and into green pastures. I want to see him who neither slumbers nor sleeps and who will supply all our needs. "Lord, show us the Father."

Jesus took this sudden, unceremonious interruption so calmly, so kindly. "Philip" — he called his disciple's name. I like a Savior who deals with each of us. Those who know him can never understand how our loving Lord is able to keep up so well with all of us. My mother-in-law in her lifetime had children residing in six or seven cities. She used to say that she would visit each one every morning in prayer and would call each name. Along that line, I knew a member in our congregation many years ago who used to say to me, "Pastor, pray for me tomorrow. Don't put me in the 'duty-bound' class," referring to our way of praying, "Lord, bless all those for whom I am duty bound to pray." Then this member would say, "Call my name, please." Well, we have a Savior who calls our name. "Philip" — that says to me that our Lord knows who we are, knows where we live, knows what our condition is, and knows what we need. I read that Jesus said, the Shepherd "calleth his own sheep by name, and leadeth them out" (John 10:3). And then he said, "I am the good shepherd, and know my sheep" (v. 14).

So Jesus answered this disciple's request by saying, "Philip, have I been so long time with you," and you do not understand? (v. 9), as if to say, "It is reasonable that those who do not know me might not understand. But how can it be that those who have been so close and experienced so much would not see how it all is?" I must stop to point out that our dullness in our relationship to God as we know him in Christ must be the greatest pain to the divine heart.

Could I make a confession to you? What I mention happens all too often to me. I will face some matter that seems greatly too much for me. I will think, examine, reflect, and picture the whole situation in my mind. Then if the matter seems insolvable and terrifying, a sense of futility and discouragement will come upon me. Only later, and it ought not to be, will I think, "Aren't you forgetting God, and that he can fix this thing?" He can make a way out of no way, and he can supply all our need. And what is worse in our slowness to lean on God is that he has delivered us over and over again. Put your name in the place of the disciple's: "Have I been so long time with you, and yet hast thou not known me, Philip?" "Philip!"

Then comes what Dr. Gossip called the most staggering statement in all literature. The words Jesus said then are the most stupendous, most gigantic, most far-reaching, most sweeping, most astonishing words ever uttered on earth: "He that hath seen me hath seen the Father." In other words, "I and my Father are one" (John 10:30). Here was this man from Nazareth, the calluses of physical labor in his hands, who would shortly face his horrible death on Calvary, and he uttered such words. And still they stand!

This is the bedrock faith of Christian believers. We have seen God in the face of Jesus Christ. He is all the God we need. In Christ, Father God is come down out of the clouds and tabernacles to where you and I live. In Jesus, Father God has made himself forever visible. In Jesus Christ, Father God has visited his lost and wandering children in a far country. In Jesus Christ, Father God has made his true makeup known to us. Christ tells us and shows us that God goes "about doing good." God in Christ heals the sick and raises the dead, gives an extra vision to the sightless, and lets deaf people hear the music of the spheres. God in Christ visits families that are mourning and sits down at feasts with those who rejoice. Christ is all the God we need. God in Christ forgives our sin. He promises to be with us in life and to come and get us in death.

I love to think of the divine sonship and power of Jesus. As someone once wrote to me in Australia,

> He was born contrary to the law of birth, and He died triumphant over the law of death. Born in poverty, wise men brought and bring their riches to the lowliness of His cradle. Born a helpless baby, He it was who spoke spinning worlds into existence and sustains the mighty pillars of the universe by His own word. He was cradled in another's crib, sailed in another's boat, rode on somebody else's animal, was buried in somebody else's tomb, and yet

to Him belong the unsearchable riches of glory. He had no possessions except a garment for which they gambled when He died, and yet the earth is His and the fullness thereof, and the cattle on a thousand hills all to Him belong. When He was an infant, He frightened a king, when He was a boy, He confused the scholars, when He was a man, He made the angry storm be still, quieted the waters, and hushed the sea until it lay down to sleep upon the bosom of His gentle command. He healed all manners of disease and charged not a penny for His service. He wrote no book, but libraries cannot hold the books written in His name, composed no music, but the noblest geniuses of melody have brought their talent and laid it at His feet. Herod could not kill Him, Satan could not seduce Him, sin could not stand Him, the roaring sea could not withstand Him, sinners could not resist Him, death could not destroy Him, and the grave could not hold Him.

He is the Rose of Sharon for those who know no loveliness, the Captain of Jehovah's host for all who are besieged, the Priest bearing our sin offering — himself.

Jesus Christ is God enough for us now, and when the journey is over, he is God enough to get us home to glory. He promises a better land than this, that somewhere there is a bright side; he promises us that somewhere God lives and all is well. Somewhere there is a land of the true where we live anew. Somewhere the load is lifted close by an open gate. Somewhere the clouds are rifted, and our burdens are laid down. Somewhere the angels sing forever, and the sabbath has no end. Somewhere the sun is shining, and the storm is all passed over. Somewhere friends meet to part no more. Oh, to trust him, Christ, our Lord and our God!

22

THE KEY TO IT ALL

John 21:15–17

So when they had dined, Jesus saith to Simon Peter, Simon, son of Jonas, lovest thou me more than these? He saith unto him, Yea, Lord; thou knowest that I love thee. He saith unto him, Feed my lambs. He saith to him again the second time, Simon, son of Jonas, lovest thou me? He saith unto him, Yea, Lord; thou knowest that I love thee. He saith unto him, Feed my sheep. He saith unto him the third time, Simon, son of Jonas, lovest thou me? Peter was grieved because he said unto him the third time, Lovest thou me? And he said unto him, Lord, thou knowest all things; thou knowest that I love thee. Jesus saith unto him, Feed my sheep. (John 21:15–17)

The subject "The Key to It All" reminded me that I have something which others of you might have. I have at my house a jar full of keys. I don't know what they fit. But I'm scared — ignorance makes me scared — to throw one of them away, for fear that I will come to a lock that has not been used, and I will not have the key. So every time I come to a lock that I have not used, and I do not know where the key is, I go through my whole jar of keys, one by one, looking for the key that will unlock that particular lock.

Life is like that. We have the notion that somewhere and somehow there is a key that will unlock the mystery of life. If we could only find the key, somewhere beyond that closed door is the answer to all of our anxieties, our uncertainties, our fears, our terrors. If only we had the right key.

Since Easter, we have together been looking at some of the postresurrection appearances of our Lord. As I recall, the Sunday after Easter I spoke to some of you about a question at night, about the fish. Have you any fish? And that comes from the same chapter from which this morning's sermon comes. And then the birthday of the church, all in that forty-day span following our

Lord's resurrection. I shall turn away after this Sunday from those scenes. But let us go back to this particular night, or morning, when our Lord sat with his disciples and ate fish that they caught and cooked — caught on the sea and cooked on the shore. And I believe that on this Mother's Day particularly it seems to me that here we have the key that will unlock the door, the key to it all!

Jesus put the question three times to Simon: "Lovest thou me? . . . Lovest thou me? . . . Lovest thou me?" And the first time he said, "Lovest thou me more than these?" Now Alexander Maclaren, I think, erred when he examined this passage. He thought that Jesus was saying, "Do you, Simon, love me more than the rest of these disciples?" But that does not strike me as fitting the makeup of our Lord. He was not pitting people, one against the other. He was not carrying on a contest. He never reduced people by making them small, certainly not those favorable to him, by comparison.

You know, all comparisons are odious. Almost all comparisons between people hurt somebody. And you and I ought to be very careful about making comparisons. It does not seem to fit the personality of our Lord. And where something occurred, or seems to occur, that does not fit a personality, does not fit a position, I think we have to take our stand on the side of what the person ordinarily or usually would do. And we ought to judge each other that way, not in terms of one act, which may have been caused by nerves or what have you, but in terms of what the total personality is like. That's the way we've got to judge each other.

I think what our Lord was really saying was, "Simon, do you love me more than all of this fishing gear that you and the rest of our friends have hauled out because they do not know what may be happening next? All of this fishing gear that you've brought out from storage, these nets, sails, and ropes; the smell of the sea and the odor of fresh-caught fish; the business that you used to be in, and seem tempted to go back to — do you love me? Do you love me more than these, these pieces of equipment that you have from your profession? Do you love me more than these?" I think that was the Lord's question to Simon.

You know, here was a man who had denied the Lord, and here Jesus faces him and asks him one question. He does not ask Simon why he failed him. He does not ask Simon to explain the environmental drag on him, which caused him to fail. He does not ask Simon about the time of the trial when he warmed himself by the fire and three times denied, the last with an oath, that he knew Jesus at all. He does not ask Simon whether it was the chill of the night that somehow unhitched him from his conviction. He does not ask him any of that. Instead Jesus comes to what I believe is the key to all of life, "Do you love me? Lovest thou me?" My friends, here is the central question, deeper than any reasoning, of whether we care or not.

A boy courts a girl, and he starts saying he doesn't like the neighborhood where she lives. He finds it difficult coming into the neighborhood. He's tired after work, or he's working late a lot of nights. You watch out because what has likely happened is that his feelings have cooled. And when people talk about how they fall off from church, from worship, and from service in the church, they give so many lies to us: "The distance is too far." "There's something about the atmosphere of the church that I don't like." "There's something about the preacher...." "Somebody said something to me that I didn't like." Well, forgive the person, or say something back to him or her. You say something everywhere else. And you ought to stop saying that you felt so hurt you just gave up. You don't give up anywhere else. If somebody makes you angry somewhere else, you just turn away or else you turn back on them, one of the two. But no, what has happened is that your love has chilled, and at least you ought to be honest about it. Your love for the Lord has cooled off. Your love for his cause is no longer warm. The temperature has gone down. Tell the truth about it, for love is the crucial answer!

So Jesus does not go into why back there Peter had denied him those three times. But he just asked, "Do you love me?" Because love does cover a multitude of sins. And if you can get that central matter straight, everything else, sooner or later, will fall in place. But if there is no true love in the relationship between God and humanity, between Christ and his servants, between people and people, between parent and child, if there's no true love, nothing finally will work out right! If I may turn this around a bit, I think the supreme virtue of true mothers has been that great capacity to love us, not just to love us when we're right, but to love us. Let me tell you that in all of these years, I think hardly two times, and I think I'm being generous, have I known a mother to say, "Well my child is just a bad person." Even when they say that, what follows is, "But...."

Once years ago, I came home tired and a little disgusted from the courts where I had been wrestling, talking to the judge about a lad. I said to my mother, "I just don't understand it. Mothers never tell me all the truth about their children. They never tell me, 'Yes, my child is just wrong.'" Listen to it on television. It doesn't matter what has happened; it doesn't matter how outrageous the crime; it doesn't matter how clear the evidence; it doesn't matter what the child's record is. When the mother is asked, she will say that he was a good boy or she was a good girl. And I said then to my mother, "I don't understand," and she said, "You would have to be a mother to understand that." But thank God for people who see something in us when nobody else sees anything worthwhile in us. You know, this is a world that turns very quickly from us. No matter what good we do, if we make one mistake, the world holds that one mistake against us.

You remember the opening lines when Shakespeare's Mark Anthony addresses his fellow citizens in the Roman forum,

> Friends, Romans, countrymen, lend me your ears;
> I come to bury Caesar, not to praise him.
> The evil that men do lives after them,
> The good is oft interred with their bones.

The world looks for what's wrong in us, but mothers look for what is right in us. And somehow mothers peer through all that's wrong and ugly and find what is decent, and they encourage us. How many of us would not be here today if somebody back yonder had not kept believing that somehow or other we had it in

us to succeed? You can make a decent life; you can be outstanding; you can have self-respect; you can make your way in life, our
mothers said. Thank God for that.

That's what Simon had in the Lord Jesus, who did not con-
demn him for what he had been or what he had done. He merely
asked him, "Do you love me? I can fix everything right if you care
about me. I can fix nothing right if you don't care about me." And
Simon gave an answer that I find of great interest. Jesus did not
put this question to Simon until they had finished eating. It says
clearly, "When they had dined...." We've got no disembodied
Christianity. Away with the people who say there is nothing to
the gospel except Jesus will save you and everything will be fine
by and by. Nothing about here and now! Jesus gave him food and
then talked to Simon about his soul.

The social gospelists may have been wrong in many things, but
we were right in believing that people's bodies have to be seen
about. There's no use talking to people about the bread of life
when their stomachs are growling. They need to get some every-
day food in their stomachs, they need to get some clothing on
their backs, they need to get a shelter over their heads, and then
they are ready to hear about the Lord Jesus. That's why I thank
God for these various projects in our church. God forbid that
either one of them would be an end within itself.

God knows that the people of Christ need to show the world
that we care about them in order to get them to care about the
Lord whom we love. So Jesus said, "Do you love me?" and
Simon, after denying him three times by a fire, now three times
by another fire, recanted: "Lord, I love you." Before, Peter said,
"I did not know him"; now, "I love you." He denied Jesus again:
"I did not know him"; now, "I love you." He said a third time, "I
did not know him," and now he says the third time, "I love you."
Then Jesus said, "I've got something for you to do. But what I've
got for you to do, you can't do unless you care about me." And
it may be that we are so weak in witnessing for Christ because
our love is weak.

I was talking the other Sunday about fire, but the fire of love will do something. It will burn inside of us, it will give us a passion, it will give us words to speak, and it will enable us to speak them in the right way. You know, sometimes somebody tells us something somebody said, and the first thing you ought to say in your mind is that you don't know how the person said it, for there are a thousand different ways to say the same thing. The trouble is that when it's reported to us, it's reported in the worst light. And it may not have been said in that light at all.

Jesus said, "I've got a job for you to do." And what does the Lord direct us to do? "Feed my sheep." There is the resurrected Christ, standing now in the full morning of his power, and his principal concern is the health of his people, "my sheep." You thought that you needed something primarily and, at last, material. Not so. The heart has reasons that reason knows not of. You and I do not live at the level of our minds; we live at the level of our hearts. The heart's findings are of the real stuff of which we are made. So Jesus said, "Feed my sheep."

And oh, my God, how people are longing to have something said to them and done for them that will give them a sense of restoration and of reconciliation, will give them a sense of footing in life. There are so many people who live with despair. There are people around you and around me who are despondent, depressed, feel abandoned, alone, helpless, weak, feel that nobody cares about them. Ah, the question is to all preachers, all Christians, do you have anything to say to anybody that will make heaven seem a little nearer to earth? Have you anything to say to anybody that will calm the raging storm in one's soul? Have you anything to say that will take away the bitterness of despair and make them feel that they are not orphans underneath an uncaring sky but they are sons and daughters of the Father's house? Have you anything to say that will lift up heads that are bowed down and dry eyes that are wet with tears? You've got it if you love the Lord. He'll give you what to say, and he'll teach you how to say it. And he'll tell you when to say it, and he'll tell you where to say it.

Now here was a poor man whose language was so crude that

he could hardly speak several sentences without cursing, but Jesus said to him, "Feed my sheep." Jesus didn't tell him *how* he was going to do it. Now here was a man whose accent was so thick that people sitting around the fire, not any scholars or masters of grammar but servant girls sitting around the fire, could tell that he came from Galilee. But Jesus said, "Feed my sheep." Never mind how you talk; never mind how guttural and harsh may be your sounds and how faulty your grammar; never mind that. "If you love me...." That's the key to it all; that's the key to life. If we love the Lord, everything else will fall into place.

Let me tell you something that I've told you before, but the true import of it did not come to me until this week. I leave this with you this morning. On May 14, 1931, my father passed out of this life. I was a boy not yet thirteen. They called me. Isn't it strange how there are some dates that we never forget? At three o'clock on a Thursday morning, they called me and told me my father was gone. My world collapsed. On that Saturday, May 16th, they buried him in Sweet Olive Cemetery in a tomb which he had already prepared for himself years before, underneath a willow tree. I never go to that place without, by day or by night, going to that cemetery and standing there before that tomb. My father's burial was on Saturday. That Sunday morning, I knocked on my mother's door. Through the door, I said, "Mother, what will we do now? How will we make it?" She didn't tell me how, but the word came back through the door, "The Lord will make a way." That was fifty-five years ago. Here was a boy coming to the storms and stresses of adolescence. Here was this poor woman with her heart broken, her husband dead, a young boy to rear. The year was 1931. Anybody that lived through the Depression will know what it was like. There was no work anywhere. Men stood on the street and sold apples and begged from door to door. A time of no work, of mortgages and debts, but through that door she said, "The Lord will make a way." I asked her, "How?" This is what came to me this week: she told me *who*. I asked her, "How?" and she told me *who*, the Lord whom she loved.

She scrimped and worked and bought no clothes for herself

in order to give me my chance. I saw her when her last kinsperson was dead, and she had no kin left within a thousand miles. Her daughter-in-law stayed and calmed her and gave her assurance and said, "You come and live with us." She didn't know how, but she knew who. I stood at her grave in the Evergreen Cemetery yesterday afternoon, and I said to her dust, "Thank you, Mother." The Lord will make a way somehow; yes, he will. I do not know how, but I know who. I've been in the storm so long now, on the sea and in the air. I don't know how I've come through, but I know who; yes, I do. I know who has brought me all this journey through. I know who, who has guided our footsteps. I know who, who has directed our pathways. I know who. I can't tell you this morning how you're going to get through whatever it is that you face, but I know who can get you safely through. I know who can pick you up when you fall down. I know who can straighten you out when you're wrong. I know who can comfort you when you're sad. I know who will be a friend when you've got no friends. I know who will dry the tears in your eyes. I know who. The Lord will make a way; oh yes, he will. The Lord will make a way, somehow. Never mind about how if you know who. Love of the Lord Christ means that "all things work together for good" — as Paul assures us in Romans 8:28.

❦ 23 ❧

A KIND ANSWER AND A SAD QUESTION

Luke 17:12–17

And as he entered into a certain village, there met him ten men that were lepers, which stood afar off: And they lifted up their voices, and said, Jesus, Master, have mercy on us. And when he saw them, he said unto them, Go show yourselves unto the priests. And it came to pass, that, as they went, they were cleansed. And one of them, when he saw that he was healed, turned back, and with a loud voice glorified God, And fell down on his face at his feet, giving him thanks: and he was a Samaritan. And Jesus answering said, Were there not ten cleansed? but where are the nine? (Luke 17:12–17)

The kind answer and the sad question in this passage both came from the lips and heart of Jesus. The event of our Lord's meeting with the ten lepers helps to establish a pattern which made up the brief time of Jesus on the earth; to state it quickly, the mood that made up so much of the Savior's life was solemn. A certain sadness seems to follow the footsteps of Jesus of Nazareth. This is to be mentioned now because it is the same solemn, grave mood which describes and characterizes the Lenten season. The conclusion ought not to be drawn that this solemnity, this sadness, was due to a natural gloominess of outlook and sourness of disposition in Jesus. There are people like that. I once knew a man who appeared to lack the ability to laugh. The closest thing to a real smile I ever saw in him was a kind of twitching of the muscles of his face. Manifestly, Jesus was not like this. We have some indirect evidence that by makeup he was of a bright and sunny spirit. Children rushed to him, and those little detectives can tell a sour apple at first sight. People do not invite killjoys to dinner parties, and Jesus was an inveterate party goer. On his own word, he wished for his friends again and again that they might know his gladness of soul, the inner brightness he had. He said it clearly once in John 15:11: "These things have I spoken unto you, that my joy might remain in you, and that your joy might be full."

The inward joy of Jesus does not cancel or hide the sadness which so marked our Lord's life that in any other it would have to be branded as tragic. We are prevented from calling the life of Jesus a tragedy only insomuch as we see in him and his work something more than what is merely human. It says something of who he was that with all which he suffered, and counting too the ignoble and ignominious way in which he died, no one speaks of the tragedy of Jesus.

Look at some of the items and elements, the events and experiences, which contributed to the pattern in Jesus of sadness and rejection which authorize one to refer to Jesus as "a man of sorrows, and acquainted with grief" (Isaiah 53:3). Look at the record. He was tempted in the wilderness, rejected in his hometown, misunderstood by his disciples, hounded by the authorities, deserted by his followers, slandered by his enemies, suspected of insanity by his own family, betrayed by a friend, tried as an outlaw, and crucified as a common criminal. He met the winter of ingratitude and knew the chill of being forsaken by those to whom he reached out a healing hand of help. Surely this is true in the case of the ten lepers, their healing and the silent departure by nine of them without a word of gratitude. Surely it ought to be, as we may draw from what Jesus said in another instance, that those who receive much, like those who are forgiven much, ought to respond greatly.

We meet in the book of Luke ten lepers who wait for Jesus to pass by in some border village between Galilee and Samaria. Samaritans and Jews had nothing to do with each other, but at least one of the lepers was a Samaritan. Luke is careful to point that out, for Luke's account in the New Testament is the supreme Gospel for the outsider, for any minority. It is Luke alone who tells us of the parable of the good Samaritan, and here it is Luke alone who tells us of ten lepers bound by their common misery into a unity which cuts across the racial and social practices of that day.

Ten men waited for Jesus with their leprosy. We do not know the exact nature of these men's sickness, for biblical leprosy included several skin diseases variously identified as contagious ringworm and psoriasis. Lepers were not shunned merely because of fear but because contact with them rendered the holy people of Israel unclean, as Leviticus 13 clearly tells us. The disease was not necessarily associated with sin, but it did mean defilement, marking the leper as unfit to be in the company of other people. When I was a lad, it was the law in our place that where someone contracted measles or mumps, a sign would be put on the house declaring that contagious disease was present in that house. These ten men knew that kind of stigma. The law of Leviticus 13:45 provided that a leper should tear his clothes as a warning to others. He was required to shave his head and to put a covering on his upper lip. He was quarantined, excluded from the community, and had to cry, "Unclean, unclean," as he approached others.

Such was the plight of ten men, one of them, at least, a Samaritan, who waited in a border village for Jesus to pass by on his last journey to Jerusalem. Misfortune does make strange comrades and pulls down many barriers. These lepers may have heard that this man from Nazareth had power over disease. He was a worker of miracles, so they waited, their hope being fought and disputed by their doubts. As Jesus passed, these lepers cried out in concert their piteous plea and their poignant prayer, "Jesus, Master, have mercy on us."

It is an appropriate cry, for all of us need mercy. Something is out of fix in all of our lives. It is one thing for you, another thing for me, but all of us have something for which we need to cry to the Lord, "Have mercy." The nation ought to lift that cry every morning. There are many noble aspirations and achievements in our American undertaking, and these ought to be gratifying to all of us, but we ought not to claim for ourselves unmixed virtue and a history which does not have elements of shame in it. We ought not to rest on the claim that we are better than other nations. The question is whether we are good enough before God. Yes, we all, singly and together, need to lift that cry, "It's me, O Lord, standing in the need of prayer."

The cry of these poor lepers attracted and arrested the attention of Jesus, our Lord. How many times from how many conditions or on how many roads had he heard that cry? He said to them, "Go show yourselves unto the priests," since the law required that the priests must declare a cure complete. It was a kind answer to a desperate plea. It was the promise of Jesus that a miracle would happen and that as they walked by faith, they would be healed by holy power. The Lord is constantly giving us kind answers with great miracles. Had you ever thought that your whole physical well-being depends on some invisible air being silently inhaled and exhaled, a breathing we forget about until under the terrible pressure of some malfunction we are panting and unable to get that invisible air into our lungs? It is a terrible thing to see such a failure of the miracle.

Do you believe in miracles? They are all around us. Your body with its incredible number of cells, functions, and interrelated actions is a miracle. We were shown on television in the case of a well-known public figure how the brain's messages are relayed to another point, which sets in motion our muscles. When that relay point fails, paralysis sets in. Think of a frail man in a lifetime wearing out eight or ten automobiles made of steel — at least they were once. That is a miracle. Do you wish to see another miracle? Look at the space beyond. Look across the street. Come inside; look around you; behold the furnishings; gaze up at these lights. Watch the activities here for a day, any day. Then look at the record of our giving. See the blank spaces. Behold the pittances for the Kingdom. It is a miracle that anything stands here, that anything goes on here. It would be a greater miracle if each of us decided to play fair with God.

As these ten lepers went, sure enough, the glow of health began to show in skin so long angry, inflamed, and diseased. They went their way rejoicing, but they forgot who had brought health again to their lives. They took the gift; they forgot the Giver. They were sincere in praying, but they were failures in praising. They were even obedient; they went as Jesus told them to do, but they were short in thanking him who blessed their lives. Only one came back to thank Jesus for his great kindness. Thus we come to one of the saddest questions ever to fall from the lips of our Lord while on earth. In his sad question, hurt can be heard, and there breathes a note of disappointment. Anyone who has tried to help and who has seen complete indifference or smug acceptance without ever a nod of acknowledgment will know something of the Savior's sad question, "Were there not ten cleansed? but where are the nine?"

Some of you may have asked the Lord to deliver you, and you promised that you would be his and he yours forever if he would only deliver you. He answered, and now you have gone on as if you never asked. Some of you were sick and asked the Lord to please have mercy and put you on your feet. He answered your prayer and you got up, but you walked away without ever a backward glance. Do I speak to someone who pleaded with the Lord to help with the children? He heard you, and now they are doing well. But you've gone on as if you never asked. Where are the young people who have been helped by the church in the name of the Lord? Where are the nine?

One, thank God, a Samaritan, came back to give thanks. Jesus said to the Samaritan, "You can really go on your way now. Your faith has made you whole" (v. 19, author's paraphrase). By inference, the others were sound in body, but this returning, thankful one was made whole, a full person, registered in the divine memory, listed in the Lamb's fair book of life.

One cannot help catching in this one Samaritan who returned a certain glad "Hallelujah," a kind of hurrah for Jesus! What a moment when we know we've laid our burden down! Some of you can remember the time when it became clear that the Lord had healed you, delivered you, blessed you, put you on your feet! "And one of them, when he saw that he was healed, turned back, and with a loud voice glorified God."

That is all we can do for the Lord — glorify him. Martin Luther spoke truly when he preached from this text. The right worship of God is to "return glorifying God with a loud voice." God stands in need of nothing else. We have nothing else to give him. The earth is his. The fiftieth psalm tells us that God allows sacrifices like a father receiving a Christmas gift from a child who has nothing of its own. The earth is his; we cannot give it to God; "the cattle upon a thousand hills" are his (Psalm 50:10). We can praise him and thank him and glorify him. We can glorify God for the sky over our head, the earth beneath our feet, the heartbeat within us, the table prepared for us. He is a Sun ever shining, a Manna ever filling, a Father ever giving, a God ever blessing, and a Fountain never failing.

God gave us Jesus, and we may be thankful for him who came a long journey looking for us and who in our lostness finds us, who in our hunger feeds us, who in our weakness strengthens us, who in our troubles delivers us, who in our sickness heals us, who in our loneliness befriends us, who in our hope confirms us, and who in our dying saves us. Praise God for Jesus!

✑ 24 ✑

Prayer of Thanksgiving

Habakkuk 3:2

O Lord, revive thy work in the midst of the years, in the midst of the years make known. (Habakkuk 3:2)

I was a fully grown man before I realized that it was a mistake to call the books of the twelve prophets whose writings bring the Old Testament to its close "minor prophets." I was a fully grown man before I realized it was a mistake. Where in the Bible short of Calvary does one come upon a picture of the love of God more touching than in the parable of the likeness of Hosea's love for his sluttish wife Gomer? Where are there more noble words about fairness among men than in the book of Amos? "Let judgment run down as waters, and righteousness as a mighty stream." How often were those words upon the lips of Martin Luther King Jr.!

Will we find anywhere in all of the biblical literature a more complete, yet so succinct and so compact, statement of our obligation before God than we will find in the book of Micah? Across the chasm of all these years, I can hear my father preaching from that text. "And what doth the Lord require of thee, but to do justly, and to love mercy, and to walk humbly with thy God?" We marched towards the building of this structure under the banner, so to speak, of words that came from the book of Haggai: "The glory of this latter house shall be greater than of the former." And where have we anywhere in Scripture a statement so concise and yet so clear about our duty, our monetary duty, our fiscal duty, our financial obligation to God, than in the words quoted here from Sunday to Sunday? "Bring ye all the tithes into the storehouse, that there may be meat in mine house, and prove me now herewith, saith the Lord of hosts, if I will not open you the windows of heaven, and pour you out a blessing, that there shall not be room enough to receive it." All of this comes from those we call the minor prophets. Now, of course, if those who so describe them in generations past meant that their writings were shorter than the longer prophets Ezekiel, Jeremiah, and Isaiah, then well and good. But if they were talking about quality, there's no way to call these minor prophets.

Our book of the morning is Habakkuk. The name is hardly pronounceable by many Christian people. In Habakkuk we come across words written maybe six hundred years before the birth of Christ that rang again in the book of Romans in the first chapter and again in the book of Galatians and again by Martin Luther some twenty-one hundred years after they were first written. The just shall live not by ceremony; the just shall live not by trades and not by the passing, the swinging, of incense; but "the just shall live by . . . faith." From this same book Habakkuk come these familiar words: "The LORD is in his holy temple: let all the earth keep silence before him." Minor prophets!

My text for the morning is a part of the second verse of the third chapter of the prophet Habakkuk: "O LORD, revive thy work in the midst of the years, in the midst of the years make known." I take that "make known" to be — how do the grammarians put it? — elliptical. That is, "make known" is understood to be "make known thy self," "make known thy power," "make known thy goodness," "make known thy mercy," "make known thy deliverance." This book of Habakkuk deals with what the theologians call "theodicy," that is, justifying the ways of God to us, making God's doings intelligible and acceptable to people. And it runs all through the prophet's thoughts. You have engaged in theodicy when you ask, "Why does God do this? Why does God allow this to happen to me?" That's theodicy: justifying the ways of God to humankind. And it runs all through Habakkuk. Why does God seem to let evil reign? not just to survive but to thrive? Why does it so often seem to have the upper hand? If it is the case that God allows evil to be and he is able to stop it, then God is powerful but not fair. If he would stop it but cannot, then God is just but not all-powerful. That is the dilemma of theodicy. If God is able but allows evil to exist, then he's not kind. If God cannot keep evil from thriving, then he is not all-powerful.

It is this question that Habakkuk wrestles with. And wrestle he does. At one point the prophet says, "I will take my watch up in my tower and see...." In other words, he wants to see why God allows disaster or peril to happen. At another point Habakkuk declares that one day the glory of the Lord will cover the earth as the waters cover the sea. Somewhere in the middle between these two extremes, between "Why does God?" and "Thank you, Lord," between the question and the answer, lies the middle passage. We hear it between Habakkuk's early question "Why do you do it?" and his later cry that the Lord will triumph. The prophet has to travel the distance between what he believes and what will take place. There in the middle years, we find, "Revive thy work in the midst of the years."

Oh, almost all of us believe that God will triumph, and yet dreadful things happen all around us. We believe that God will triumph; it's sort of cut into our being that somehow or the other goodness will prevail. Disappointments are not able for most of us to wipe what is right out, for somehow things will turn out all right. James Russell Lowell wrote as the clouds of civil conflict gathered ever darker over the land; he looked out at the awful evil of slavery. You remember the familiar words, "Truth forever on the scaffold, Wrong forever on the throne. Yet the scaffold sways the future, and in the dim unknown standeth God within the shadow keeping watch over his own." It's textured into us, somehow goodness will win! Many people who have no profound religious trust still believe that somehow goodness will overcome. I knew a man in years gone by named Bernie Resnick. He said to me, as I often recall, that he had no particular religious faith. Yet Bernie Resnick, in the Urban League of Brooklyn, in the Urban League of New York, twenty-five, thirty years ago, spent his life and strength in the interest of better housing, quality education, and equal opportunity. He had no religious faith, but there was in him somehow or other...I cannot explain it; maybe it was a residue, or carryover, a kind of appendage from some past generation of his forebears, but there was in him the belief that he ought to serve the cause of goodness and right and truth. He had no discernible religious faith. Clarence Darrow, a great criminal lawyer, declared himself to be an atheist but spent his years, many of them, defending unpopular causes.

Well, of course, you and I who are Christians have no choice except to trust and believe and to have confidence. We have no choice but to have confidence that the cause of God will triumph, because to give that up is to give up being a Christian. You and I stand on the Monday-morning side of resurrection Sunday, the Monday-morning side, you understand, of resurrection Sunday. You and I have the pivotal events of our salvation history upon which our faith is founded — crucifixion and resurrection. We cannot doubt that truth crushed to earth will rise again. We have seen truth incarnate, truth in flesh, crushed to earth and rise again. We have passed from Friday to Sunday; we have seen the "no-power" of Friday translated into the "all-power" of Sunday morning. We have no choice except to believe that God's cause will triumph.

James Stewart said that the crowd that gathered against Jesus on Calvary was the most sinister coalition of evil ever assembled on earth. When men had said all the "no" they could to God on Friday, God said "yes" on Sunday morning. Thanks be to God, the "no" got wiped out. The "yes" rings out in the "Hallelujah Chorus": "And he shall reign forever and ever, King of kings and Lord of lords." We have no choice; not to trust is to give up being a Christian, for we stand on the Monday-morning side of resurrection Sunday. He will be all and all; the last enemy to be destroyed is death. When the grim final enemy has stepped down from the ranks of darkness and challenged the Son of God for the last time and has finally been put down, destroyed, our Lord, Paul tells us, is to deliver up the kingdom to God the Father that he might be all in all. But in the meantime, dreadful things go on. Bad news comes. It isn't an easy pilgrimage we have to make. Oh yes! God is going to win, but we are in the middle of the years now. We stand in between where we start out and what is finally to happen. And sometimes the news gets awfully bad.

At Dartmouth last week, the school from which Daniel Webster graduated in 1801, a new crop of conservative students took sledgehammers and tore down the symbols of opposition to apartheid in South Africa. This happened in one of our greatest institutions. What shall we say? One of the few voices in South Africa raised against apartheid has been that of Marly Blackburn, who strangely enough died in an automobile accident. Bad news comes every week, every day. Take the little inland surrounded country of Lesotho. I preached once in Lesotho, and our World-Wide Guild sent a set of the *Interpreter's Bible* there. Well, Lesotho, pressed by the South African blockade, collapsed, had to succumb, had to bow down to South African pressure; it's not an easy fight.

Those of you who watched Bill Moyers last night cannot help feeling the grim outlook before us. Sixty percent of our black children are born out of wedlock. Fifty percent of the prison population of America today is black, fifty percent! I heard even more startling figures. A University of Chicago survey, Bill Moyers said, gives a terrifying prospect. Back in the 1960s when Daniel Moynihan first spoke about the crisis of the black family, many of us were outraged; I was. I apologize to Senator Moynihan this morning. He was right; it is a major crisis. That University of Chicago survey, Bill Moyers said last night, predicts that by the year 2000, if we continue along our present way, 70 percent of our children will be in single-parent families. How we do need to pray in the midst of the years, "Make known thy power. O Lord, revive thy work in the midst of the years. Give us some new strength, some new hope, some new direction, some new light on our pathway. O Lord, revive thy work in the midst of the years."

I never like to keep things on a broad scale. It is so in each of our lives when we start out, of course, that we have questions. But we have an enthusiasm; we have a verve and zest and a notion of what we can do and what we can be. The world is our oyster, and we're ready for the handling of it. Everything seems to be on our side. The tide flows in our favor. We move in strength, and though our vision may be warped, we have a vision of a world that might be and can be, and we believe, many of us, that we can help bring it to pass. But in the middle of the years, which has nothing to do with a particular age but with having started out and having found out how strong the entrenchments of evil are, having found that out, something begins to take root inside of us. There are Christian people who started out with a great enthusiasm; they thought the habits they had would fall down before their prayers, their first prayers, and they felt that all the road would be smooth before them because now they had accepted Jesus Christ. But in the midst of the years, we find out it's not quite that way. The tide turns against us, our strength weakens. We begin to wonder if our strength is enough to meet the trials of the world. Friends disappear around us. Jealousy seeps into our companionships; things go wrong in our prayers; we get off schedule. It's the third quarter, we're behind, and it doesn't look like we can catch up before the final whistle!

What is there to do when our own strength gives out? when we know that we do not have the reserves to match the odds up against which our lives are met? What can we do but ask, "O Lord, revive our work in the midst of the years; in the midst of the years make known thy goodness, make known thy power, make known thy love, rescue us from despair, deliver us from fear"? This ought to be our prayer now. These are difficult days; they grow more difficult for many of us. But thanks be to God, we have somewhere we can turn. Yes, one day, his word, his spirit, will cover the earth, but right now in the midst of our struggles when we're knocked down and bruised and bleeding, we can pray unto him, "O Lord, revive thy work, raise up my bowed-down head, dry my weeping eye, and renew my strength." Thanks be to God that they that so cry have the assurance that "the LORD shall renew their strength; they shall mount up with wings as eagles; they shall run, and not be weary; and they shall walk, and not faint." Call him, ask him to help. When strength gives out, ask him to give you strength.

When it looks as if we cannot go on another day, ask him to be still our strength and shield. Revive thy work. Stand by me; stand by me. When the world is tossing me like a ship upon the sea, thou who rulest wind and water, stand by me. He will give his angels charge over you to keep you in all your ways. They will bear you up in their arms. O Lord, revive thy work. Give us the vision we had when we started out. O Lord, revive thy work; help us to go on to climb high mountains. O Lord, revive thy work, give us strength, give us hope, and give us faith. To whom else can you turn? To whom else can I turn? Where else is there to look? "O LORD, revive thy work in the midst of the years."

❧ 25 ❧

THE SONG OF MOSES AND THE SONG OF THE LAMB

Exodus 15:2–3,7; Revelation 15:1–3

The LORD is my strength and song, and he is become my salvation: he is my God, and I will prepare him an habitation; my father's God, and I will exalt him. The LORD is a man of war: the LORD is his name.... And in the greatness of thine excellency thou hast overthrown them that rose up against thee. (Exodus 15:2–3,7)

And I saw another sign in heaven, great and marvelous, seven angels having the seven last plagues; for in them is filled up the wrath of God. And I saw as it were a sea of glass mingled with fire: and them that had gotten the victory over the beast, and over his image, and over his mark, and over the number of his name, stand on the sea of glass, having the harps of God. And they sing the song of Moses the servant of God, and the song of the Lamb, saying, Great and marvelous are thy works, Lord God Almighty; just and true are thy ways, thou King of saints. (Revelation 15:1–3)

I want to talk with you a little while tonight on the song of Moses and the song of the Lamb. Our Scripture is from the fifteenth chapter of Revelation, beginning at the first verse.

What words are here in the midst of all the bright visions and the sounds of the trumpets and the harps and the music that all go to make up the last book of the Bible! These words talk about music; they sing the song of Moses and the song of the Lamb.

Sitting here tonight listening to these choirs, I thought to myself how poor the faith would be if we did not have any music. The church has marched for twenty centuries to the drumbeat of its music. When a new black religious movement swept through America twenty-five years ago, I said to a young black Mennonite scholar, "This movement will not go very far." He was a little put out, I think, by that comment because many young blacks were fascinated with this new movement which was sweeping

155

through the country. And I said, it will not go very far because it does not have any music, for nothing can march long and well without music.

There are all kinds of music. There is the sorrow music of our forebears, the spirituals and their work songs, and then there's the music of disappointed love that we hear in the blues. But music, music is the language which the soul turns to when ordinary speech will not carry the weight of what is felt. Music comes out when there isn't anything to say that you can say in ordinary sentences. It is the language of the soul when it is stretched — music is. Joseph Sittler at the University of Chicago Divinity School said some years ago that when you hear the music of Handel, as in the *Messiah,* which we all hear so much of these days at Easter, you hear the well-ordered life, the calm and peaceful melody, of eighteenth-century England where everything seemed in order. So it's a lilting music. It has no jarring sounds; it just sort of surges along. But when you hear the music of our own young musicians out of the ghetto and out of the hurt of black life, there is sometimes a violence in the music, you know, and a scream in it. Max Roach, the drummer, is a member of my congregation, and he said to me, "Yes, this is true," because the emotions of the ghetto, the black community, are sometimes raw and hurting, and that comes out in the music.

Well, this music that we hear — the song of Moses and the song of the Lamb — comes out of a struggle and a deliverance from a struggle. Somebody has been trapped and has got loose, and music is the result of the deliverance. In the first instance, the children of Israel have left Egypt; they have flung across their shoulders what they are able to carry, and they've started out on the long journey toward the land of promise. The Egyptians, following the afflictions that have fallen upon them, decide to let them go. But when the economists of Pharaoh began totaling up what they were losing in this free slave labor, they decided they would rather have the afflictions than to lose this free labor. And so the Egyptians started out after the children of Israel in order to bring them back, because slave owners never really give up.

They don't give up because they believe they can't afford to give up. In the free market, cheap labor is too important to slave masters for them to turn it loose freely. They may turn it loose when they have to, but they'd like to get it back. And so the armies of Egypt — following the findings of their economists about how the Egyptian economy might go to pieces, having lost all their free labor — march after their slaves to get them back. Evil does not give up easily.

A lot of us have made a mistake about that. We thought that the Voting Rights Act and the like would solve our problems of race. Well, I read in the New Orleans paper last night that a state senator was complaining in Jefferson parish yesterday or one day this week about the harm of integration and was really talking about trying to get back to what they used to have. And so the armies of Egypt pursued, trying to get back what they had given up because evil does not give up easily. It fights on and on. There are a lot of great problems that keep recurring. We are facing something now in this country, and many people are blind to it. I've spoken up and down the country, and others have, too, and many people are blind to this, but we ought to at least be aware of it. What we have going on in the country today is a marriage. . . . It is not really a marriage; I ought not honor it that way. It is an ugly liaison, a "shacking up" between the political right and the religious right. The flag wavers and the Bible beaters have got together now. Some of them are on television, and some of you watch them, but they are together. They don't talk about the Lord much, but they talk a great deal about the president — Sunday after Sunday. Some of them originate from places whose names are appropriate to what they are really about — like Lynchburg. And they have joined hands with the political right led by a charming man, who was really a better actor as president than he was as an actor. I don't mean to talk against the president because as old as I am, I respect anybody who is older than I am. They have joined hands, and their purposes are on the side, not of more freedom, but less freedom — this is their purpose, and we ought to at least know what's happening. And all the while, they are selling the country to foreign interests. Take General Motors for instance, about which Charles Wilson once said, "What is good for General Motors is good for America." But General Motors, our biggest automobile maker, is now a junior partner of the Japanese maker Toyota. Junior partner. All the while they are selling the country out to foreign interests, selling it out. Essex House in New York today belongs to foreign people. Canon electronics, all to foreign people. Evil does not give up easily. Like Mardi Gras time, it keeps changing masks. It's hard to tell who it is because they put down one mask and pick up another. It's the same crowd. And no matter what mask they put on, it's the same people behind the mask. Evil does not give up easily.

Let me not talk only about what other people are doing to us. I must also talk about what we are doing to ourselves. Sixty percent of our black children are born now to single-parent families. Fifty percent of the prison population of America today is made up of black people. I am not talking now about the injustice — yes, it is there — I am talking about how we destroy ourselves. The University of Chicago has projected that, by the year 2000, 70 percent of our black children will be born into single-parent families. Only 30 percent of black males in America will be employed. I am talking about the destruction of a race. As someone said to me Sunday night, a great deal of our problem is not just that there are single parents, but it is that our parents are so selfish and concerned about themselves that they take no interest in their children. Evil does not give up easily.

The armies of Egypt came on behind this pilgrim band of Israel. And the people could hear at the back of the ranks at first a kind of low indistinct sound, a murmur back in the distance behind them. But as those chariot wheels rang against the rocks, that threatening murmur grew into a louder volume until finally it was a thunder and a terrified cry went up from the rear ranks of the Israelites, "The Egyptians are coming. The Egyptians are coming." It went from rank to rank until it got up to where Moses was. "The Egyptians are coming." There God's people stood, precipitous walls on both sides with a sea before them which they had no means to cross, and behind them, the growing thunder of an angry host as the chariots of Pharaoh pursued and drew ever closer to the rear ranks. Moses in consternation wondered what he would do. The Lord said to him, "What is that in your hand?" "Nothing but a shepherd's staff." "Well, use it!"

The Lord requires that we use whatever we've got. He said, "Use that." If my talents are not what yours are, I'm not exempt from using them. "Use that!" That's all God wants — use what you've got! Do something! For God's sake, do something! Moses stretched out the staff. Now how foolish that was. But that is all right. The power is not in the staff anyhow; it's in Moses's willingness to commit what he had to God — that's all. Never mind what your talent is; it isn't enough. There never has been a talent large enough to meet the need, but God asks that that which you have be thrown in on his side. The decisiveness is not in how much you've got; it's in what God will do with what you've got. He can take hardly anything and make everything out of it. He can take a few loaves and some fish and feed five thousand people. I look back at my life now and what the Lord has done with it — I am amazed myself! All the Lord asks is, "Give me what you've got. Put yourself in my hands. Let me have charge of your life. Let me use you. Give me what you've got. I'll make out of it what I want." There was Moses with nothing but a stick, not a thing to it, just a piece of wood. Use it for God's sake. Do something. Do something. As Moses stretched out the staff, God went into action — that's where the difference is anyhow. It's not in us; it's in the Lord. "Except the LORD build the house" — the workmen can work on it day and night, but it will never be properly fixed up. The Lord must see to its building.

If you and I are ever going to be right, it's because the Lord fixes us. It takes the Lord to straighten us out. Takes the Lord to pick us up. Takes the Lord to put us on the right road. Takes the Lord to put a song in our hearts. And so as Moses took that little nothing of a piece of wood, a little stick, God went into action. The waters of the sea began backing up. Winds divided — one wind went one way; another wind went the other way. They were

God's winds. God's winds. God's water. Somebody asks, "Did it happen?" Well, the greatest race of spiritual geniuses the world has ever seen has built itself for three thousand years upon it having happened. Israel has been persecuted in every land, but the Jews have gone on, and they trace their foundation to what happened at that Red Sea. The waters backed up; not only that but God dried out the wet seabed. They started down in the seabed and marched on through. Then they stood on the far side of the sea and started shaking the dust from their sandals that would never grow old until they got in the Promised Land. They shook the dust from their sandals, and Moses sang a song to God. They said, "The LORD is my strength and song, and he has become my salvation.... The LORD is a man of war: the LORD is his name ... hast overthrown them that rose up against thee." This is the song of Moses. It is the song of deliverance here, now, in this world, not off in some distant future. The Lord delivers us now. He will pick us up when we're down now; he will straighten us out when we're wrong now. He will strengthen us when we are weak now. He will help us when we cry out now. He will answer us when we pray now. Now!

But then, there's the song of the Lamb. The song of Moses is the song of God acting in human affairs, acting where people do wrong and where people try to do right. That's one struggle, but there's another struggle going on. It's a mighty universal struggle, and it surrounds our little struggle. It is that huge struggle which gives cue and clue to our little struggle. Something, somebody, is lined up against God. Mighty powers. How does Paul put it? "We wrestle not against flesh and blood, but against principalities, against powers, against the rulers of the darkness of this world, against spiritual wickedness in high places." We war not against flesh and blood, but there is some great struggle going on in the universe. Put it how you want: the struggle between light and darkness, between life and death, goes on in your body and mine right now, between health and sickness, between good and bad, between right and wrong, between God and Satan. There's a battle, a mighty battle, raging through the universe, and evil in that battle is not weak. I hear my Lord on the night of his arrest saying to those who came to arrest him, "This is your hour and the power of darkness." And is it not recorded in the Scripture somewhere that scarcely shall the righteous be saved? It's not an easy fight. Ah, young preachers, you will not put to rout the armies of the aliens the first nor very likely the last time you stand up. Your job is to witness to the Lord. There is a mighty struggle going on, and the Bible speaks about that struggle in many ways. It is strange, puzzling language really. Somewhere in the First Testament is a word: "How art thou fallen from heaven, O Lucifer" (Isaiah 14:12). And in the book of Revelation there is a strange word of a red dragon who comes plunging from the heavens and pulls a third of creation down with it (Revelation 12:3–4).

There's a mighty war going on. How will it come out? Who is going to win? Well, those of us who are Christians have peeked at the last page. Remember those old books — arithmetic books and whatnot — where the answers were in the back? We've had a chance to peek at the last page. When Friday morning began, we got a sign of what's going to happen. The most powerful coalition of evil ever assembled on the face of this earth came together at Calvary, and they threw up all of their battlements and all of their armory against the Son of God. It was a mighty battle, an awful tussle; the earth watching it grew sick at how evil could challenge the very throne of God. The world shivered on its axis and trembled on its foundation. The heavens looked down at it and grew dark because they mourned at seeing evil standing up in God's face. So the curtains of darkness were pulled across the face of the sunlight because the heavens would not watch it. Angels that sing around God's throne grew suddenly silent, and somebody wrote that there was silence in heaven for about the space of a half hour. It looked for a little while as if God had lost. I hear that awful cry trembling up from that hill underneath a darkened sky — midnight at midday. I hear that awful cry, "My God, my God, why hath thou forsaken me?" It looked like God had lost, but when the light came back on and the earth had righted itself, God's grip held and hell's grip loosened. Jesus cried out, "It is finished." The old account is settled. It has all been straightened out, fixed, settled; the disease has been cured. I know how it's going to come out. I do not know when, but somewhere in God's own time, evil is going to bow down before the Lord. Somewhere and somehow, all that is wrong will be made right. Somewhere and somehow in God's own time, every valley will be lifted up, every mountain will be brought down, every crooked way will be made straight, every rough way will be made plain in God's own time. Sickness and sorrow, pain and death, we will fear no more. In God's own time, the clouds will pass away. In God's own time, the sun will shine in an unclouded sky. In God's own time!

⌣ 26 ⌣

The Soul's Desperate Plea

Psalm 19

> The heavens declare the glory of God; ...
> The law of the Lord is perfect, ...
> Keep back thy servant also from presumptuous sins; ...
> (Psalm 19:1,7,13)

Two of the principal aspects of worship are praise and petition. Praise is adoration growing out of the recognition of the greatness and goodness of God. It is exultation, triumphant, surging, set to gladsome music. Praise is worship with sunshine upon it. Poor indeed is any service which calls itself Christian and which does not have in it a large place for praising God for what he is and for what he does. Threadbare is any prayer meeting, public or private, which does not have a large place for praising God for his loving-kindness and tender mercy. Praise is the Christian's native air, the true climate of his soul. Praise is the soul's instinctive language, its natural music. "It is good to sing praises unto our God; for it is pleasant; and praise is comely" (Psalm 147:1).

The praise of God is not founded upon the fact that he gives us everything we want. Praise grows out of awareness that God is great and good, great and good when we get what we want, great and good when we are denied the askings of our heart. There is a telling and memorable scene in the twenty-ninth chapter of 1 Chronicles. King David was old; his days were numbered. He had long wanted to build the temple of God on Mount Zion. This chief ambition had eluded David, and he recognized that he would never achieve his goal. Calling together the leaders of the nation, he announced that he would not build the temple, but Solomon, his son, would. Then David, though disappointed, led the nation in an offering to God. At its conclusion he sounded the note of praise in these words:

> Blessed be thou, LORD God of Israel our Father, for ever and ever. Thine, O LORD, is the greatness, and the power, and the glory, and the victory, and the majesty: for all that is in the heaven and in the earth is thine; thine is the kingdom, O LORD.... Both riches and honour come of thee,... and in thine hand is power and might; and in thine hand it is to make great, and to give strength unto all. Now therefore, our God, we thank thee, and praise thy glorious name. (1 Chronicles 29:10–13)

Immediately, however, David's mind and heart turned to his and the people's weakness: "But who am I, and what is my people, that we should be able to offer so willingly after this sort? for all things come of thee, and of thine own have we given thee. For we are strangers before thee, and sojourners, as were all our fathers" (vv. 14–15). Toward the end of his prayer, David broke into unmistakable pleading, "Keep this for ever in the imagination of the thoughts of the heart of thy people, and prepare their heart unto thee: And give unto Solomon my son a perfect heart" (vv. 18–19).

So joined to praise is petition, pleading, growing out of an awareness of our own weakness and wickedness made glaring and unbearable because we have seen the King in his glory, in his greatness, and in his goodness. The arrogance of people grows out of a flat-topped view of life. We look over, and we look down, but we do not look up. Americans would be, I believe, far more serious and far more sincere about this idea of democracy if we really stopped to ponder the grandeur and splendor of the principles upon which the nation is founded. Granted all of the contradictions of slavery and what has followed, dark and tragic as it is, still one must say that the notion "all men are created equal" is a daring, bold leap. My Harvard colleague Professor Ewart Guinier said in my hearing at Cambridge that, given the institution of slavery, how often must the writers and reviewers of our Declaration of Independence have been tempted to say, "We hold these truths to be self-evident; that all men are created equal; except, except, except...." And yet they did not. We would be a better people if we measured ourselves against the grandeur of the idea of democracy.

When one looks at God's greatness and our smallness, praise must break forth, to be followed by the soul's desperate plea to be established in our going out and our coming in. When we truly consider God's goodness and our selfishness, praise bursts out, but that very praise makes us want to plead that our steps might be ordered of the Lord. When we look at Jesus and what he has done for us poor undeserving people, we cannot help praising his name and at the same time crying out, "Have mercy, Lord. Have mercy!"

It is these twins of praise and petition which make the writer of the nineteenth psalm a spokesman for all of us. It is these twins of praise and petition which make the nineteenth a perennially touching prayer and an immortal article of worship, whose words and phrases are etched into the consciousness and conscience of generations without number. The praise of the psalmist is aimed at two aspects of the works and wonders of God: the glory of nature and the grandeur of his love. There are biblical scholars who hold that we have here the work of two psalmists. With this I do not agree; it seems thoroughly in order that the one man would consider and praise the handiwork of God in nature and the solemn ordinances and laws of God operating in the whole universe. Immanuel Kant in *Critique of Pure Reason* does the same thing, referring "to the starry heavens above...and the moral law within."

The psalmist was moved with awe and adoration as his eyes and mind swept the vast and starry skies. As he looked north, south, east, and west and beheld the fiery hosts of blazing stars and considered the flaming sun, he cried, "The heavens declare the glory of God; and the firmament showeth his handiwork." Let me retire for a moment and let the psalmist speak for himself via the printed page as he praises God for his handiwork in the distant stars. He said that the creature is praising the Creator in the heavenly bodies. When the psalmist looked at the great orbs of fire burning in the canopy of the sky, he realized how noble must be the mind which conceived and executed the wonder and beauty of the firmament. The psalmist said, "The heavens are telling the glory of God" (RSV), and the firmament is the first of the voices of glory praising the greatness of God. What a vast theme! What a noble meditation! The heavens speak of beauty, of vastness, and of a steadfast order held together by the creative genius of the God of us all.

I have gone too far. Let me acknowledge the psalmist. He said, "Day unto day uttereth speech." In other words, a day marches out of its secret dwelling place, plays its part in the unfolding panorama of God's eternal purpose, quietly exits to make room for another day, and as it departs, whispers to its successor that God is glorious and wonderful. Let the psalmist talk on; I like the way he goes about it: "Night unto night showeth knowledge." As evening falls, the gloaming comes, and night stretches its sable shroud over a pausing and resting earth; each night proclaims, "God is great," and as it departs passes a great trumpet to its successor that it might declare also the glory of God.

Let the psalmist talk on. He declared that God has made the skies as "a tabernacle for the sun" and, no less effectively because he spoke in pre-Copernican terms, that the sun praises God by coming forth joyous and hopeful each succeeding day like a bridegroom from his chambers, starting his journey fresh and unwearied as an athlete, "and rejoiceth as a strong man to run a race." Praise God for the glories of nature!

Quickly the psalmist then turned to God's law and shifted his rhythm to a precise and careful structure. God is glorified in his Law: "The law of the LORD is perfect." It is sufficient to live by. It revives the soul; it establishes our going and our coming. The law of the Lord as given by Jesus is indeed perfect: "Thou shalt love the Lord thy God with all thy heart, and with all thy soul, and with all thy mind.... And... Thou shalt love thy neighbour as thyself" (Matthew 22:37–38). Let that blessed day come when all people shall obey that law and we may open every prison, unlock every door, and walk every street in safety.

Let the psalmist talk on! "The testimony of the LORD is sure, making wise the simple," so that a fool need not err in the way. Yes, "The fear of the LORD is clean, enduring for ever." God's law does not change. Situational ethics is a concession to our wickedness and our shortsightedness, but let me say loud and clear, God's law does *not* change for you or for me. Let it be said, God's law remains forever the same: truth is forever true, lying is forever false, adultery is forever wrong, selfishness is forever destructive, drunkenness is forever self-defeating, and peacemaking is forever kin to God.

Beholding and praising the greatness of God in nature and in his law, the psalmist cried out, "Cleanse thou me from secret faults." Did he mean faults which others cannot see? Or did he mean those faults which we do not see in ourselves? There are deep failures in us hidden from our own awareness: "There is a way," the Bible says twice, "which seemeth right unto a man, but the end thereof are the ways of death" (Proverbs 14:12; 16:25). "Cleanse thou me from secret faults," from following my own way, and save me from misunderstanding what God has said in the Bible and in my life. Save me from going off after half-truths, half-lie cults, and manmade movements, for people "heap to themselves teachers, having itching ears" (2 Timothy 4:3).

On went the psalmist: "Keep back thy servant also from presumptuous sins." Let me not go too far. God is merciful, but let me not take too much for granted in his goodness. God will protect us, but let us not tempt him in our waywardness. Let me not go too far. Stop me short of the horrible pit — that fatal step.

And then the peak of the plea: "Let the words of my mouth, and the meditation of my heart, be acceptable in thy sight." Do you not want, long, yearn to move in, the God climate? I do yearn to breathe in the God atmosphere, long for that posture of the soul where sin and sense molest no more, heaven comes down our souls to greet, and glory crowns the mercy seat. Do you not long to move in the God way? I do. Let my words and my thoughts be God centered. Let my hopes be God founded. Let us walk in the God way, talk God talk, think God's thoughts, sing God's songs, and live in God's sight. "Let the words of my mouth, and the meditation of my heart, be acceptable in thy sight," until God is all around us, all over us, all under us, all through us, all behind us, all before us, until God is all in all, and we are caught up to meet him.

✧ 27 ✧

SPIRITUAL SUCCESS

Psalm 16:8

I have set the LORD always before me: because he is at my right hand, I shall not be moved. (Psalm 16:8)

When someone has achieved something noteworthy, one of the first questions put to that person inquires how the success was attained. When a man or a woman reaches an unusually advanced age, reporters want to know, "How did you live to be a hundred or a hundred and five?" The oldster knows that a kind of game is being played since one does not usually get old without learning at least a few things, though young people can rarely understand this. So with a merry twinkle in the eye, the senior citizen supplies the reporter with something spicy, "I believe that I have lived as long as I have because I drink a jigger of gin every morning and have done so for sixty or seventy years." The oldster winks, and the reporter smiles knowingly as if the two share an exciting secret which will make good reading in the morning newspaper.

There was a time when this explanation of how one reaches a great age varied a little if the old person was female and black. Laughing broadly, the old black lady would squint a bit, throw back her head, and then with a toothless laugh declare that she got so old because she smoked her corncob pipe every day since she was a teenager. The next day the old lady's picture would appear in the newspaper, and she would be seen by all sitting in her rocking chair on the porch and smoking her corncob pipe. We've made some interesting allowances in what we approved and in what we frowned upon in past generations. Nobody criticized or condemned old ladies for smoking corncob pipes. In my childhood I knew many matriarchs — mothers of the church, as we called them — who smoked their corncob pipes without any hint

168

of criticism. But while old ladies could smoke their corncob pipes without criticism, it was a scandal and an outrage for a young woman to smoke a cigarette. She was going to hell for sure. I am not out to prove anything, but this was an interesting difference made by our elders.

The curiosity about how something is achieved is not confined to queries to the old. The successful businessperson is asked over and over as to what he or she attributes the great achievement. The athlete is asked endlessly to explain what it was that made him or her so supremely skillful in that champion's particular sport. We want to know partly out of sheer curiosity and partly because we believe that we, too, may be able to find the combination of victory and the secret of success.

The same mood and practice exist in the area of things which touch our spirits. The successful artist is constantly studied with the hope that the *how* may be found out. Let a preacher attain any eminence in pulpit work, and such a one will be bombarded in conferences and seminars times without number as to how it is done. The best human answer is that technique can be taught; art cannot. "Whence to the poet his poetry" is an area of mystery. A master cook can give accurate recipes, though I am not sure they often do, but getting the feel to make food come out right is a different matter.

The author of the sixteenth psalm was not slow to tell us how he found spiritual power and assurance. It might well be that someone put the question to him as to the source of his strength of soul. Above everything else, this is what we want. I venture the comment that there is nothing we do which is not aimed at satisfying us spiritually. The new car? It makes us feel successful. The new clothes? They give us a sense of well-being. So we keep searching, trying on, contracting, and changing. All of this is aimed at the person within. Now, here is a man who seems calm, poised, at peace with himself, radiant with faith, his face aglow with a light which comes from neither sea nor land. The reporters crowd in upon him: tell us how it is done. And he answers, "I have set the LORD always before me: because he is at my right hand, I shall not be moved."

We do need the Lord ever before us to correct us. It is so easy for us to imagine we are what we are not, to ask so much of others and so little of ourselves, to be always accusing the next fellow and forever justifying ourselves. Dr. James Sanders, a uniquely gifted Old Testament scholar, pointed out in his book *God Has a Story, Too* that the Bible is a mirror in which we may see ourselves. Sanders said that if we read the Bible and come away self-satisfied or feeling self-righteous, we have almost surely read it wrongly. In the trial and death of Jesus, you and I are not Jesus. What sacrifice of life, or in life, have we made? We are the high priest wanting to protect our position. We are Judas deciding that Jesus has had enough time to prove himself, so we must take things into our own hand. We are Peter, afraid of public opinion around us. We are the crowd ready to dance to any tune. How dare I read that account and think of myself as being like Jesus? The spiritual does not say, "Were you crucified with my Lord?" It says, "Were you there when they crucified my Lord?" We are miles away from grasping the Scriptures until our pride is shattered and we see ourselves as loathsome creatures who by the mercy of God and the work of Christ may be made useful instruments in the hands of the Almighty.

We desperately need the presence of God to convict us of our sins and wrongs and to bring us to a godly sorrow and repentance for what we have done wrong. Like Isaiah, before God we can only sob, "I am a man of unclean lips, and I dwell in the midst of a people of unclean lips" (6:5). The writer who wrote the words "I have set the LORD always before me" might well be the same author of the words in the fifty-first psalm,

> Have mercy upon me, O God, according to thy lovingkindness: according unto the multitude of thy tender mercies. . . . I acknowledge my transgressions: and my sin is ever before me. . . . Purge me. . . . Hide thy face from my sins, and blot out all mine iniquities. Create in me a clean heart, O God; and renew a right spirit within me. Cast me not away from thy presence; and take not thy holy spirit from me. (Psalm 51:1–11)

You and I need to pray that prayer for correction, and to pray it often because we need to set the Lord always before us.

As your life and mine need correction before God, we need also to be challenged to rise higher as living souls than we have yet reached. The truest character of our humanity is to "be up and doing, / With a heart for any fate, / Still achieving, still pursuing, / Learn to labour and to wait," as Longfellow wrote. To slump and to quit, to become morally flabby and spiritually self-satisfied, is not what our humanity is all about, yet this is surely what is wrong with all too many of us.

It is a mockery of the Lord Jesus Christ who came that we might have life fully and abundantly for us to slouch down in some halfway house of the spirit. Yet there are Christians who have not grown in ten, twenty, thirty, or forty years. So many of us have no deeper spiritual life than when we were baptized. Our prayer life is still a simple, childish routine: "Now I lay me down to sleep, / I pray the Lord my soul to keep. / If I should die before I wake, / I pray the Lord my soul to take." The *I* has never broadened into *we* in our prayers. Men and women, boys and girls, our own children, our own kin, and our own friends are racing to hell, but we are not in an agony of prayer for them. Too many of us are still in the same old patterns we were in twenty or thirty years ago. We know the Lord no better, and we have no deeper fellowship now with him than we had then.

The Lord has called us to higher things. If we would set him before us, our spirits would stretch out on his promises, and our eyes would be lifted up toward the heights of godliness and saintliness: "There remaineth yet very much land to be possessed" (Joshua 13:1). We are called to be more prayerful than we are, more holy than we are. There is a note of aspiration and holy desire in the Psalms:

> Blessed is the man that walketh not in the counsel of the ungodly, nor standeth in the way of sinners, nor sitteth in the seat of the scornful. But his delight is in the law of the LORD; and in his law doth he meditate day and night. And he shall be like a tree planted by the rivers of water, that bringeth forth his fruit in his season; his leaf also shall not wither; and whatsoever he doeth shall prosper. (Psalm 1:1–3)

The man who wrote these words might well be the same as the one who said, "I have set the LORD always before me."

Beyond any question, we need to be put under conviction and corrected. And to be sure, we need to be challenged so that our possibilities in God can stretch out before us. Beyond all of this, we need to be comforted in the shocks and batterings of life. One of our greatest of New Testament scholars, Dr. C. H. Dodd said that as the years came and went, he found a much greater need to be comforted in the midst of life's sorrows and its sobs. It is so! One has only to live to discover that the atmosphere changes as we go along. The morning freshness wears to blazing noonday. The afternoon prophesies of shadows and darkness.

We discover before too long that we are not strong enough. Dreams disappear or turn to ashes in our hands. The friends of the morning disappear. The way grows weary and long. The burdens press ever more heavily. More and more we find ourselves surrounded by those who do not understand us as we believe we were understood in earlier days. The footstep falters now and then, and the memory grows not so reliable as once it was. The news seems sad more often than it once did. Like Bedivere, the last of King Arthur's knights, we feel ourselves companionless, among new people, strange faces, other minds. We do need the comfort of God, for there is no other who relieves us, renews us, and restores us on this toilsome way. Keep the Lord ever before you, and you shall not be without consolation. In one of his last promises did not the Lord Jesus say, "I will not leave you comfortless"?

The psalmist who wrote our text and said, "I have set the LORD always before me," may well have been the same who was enabled by constant vision of God to write these words of infinite comfort:

> The LORD is my shepherd; I shall not want. He maketh me to lie down in green pastures: he leadeth me beside the still waters. He restoreth my soul: he leadeth me in the paths of righteousness for his name's sake. Yea, though I walk through the valley of the shadow of death, I will fear no evil: for thou art with me; thy rod

and thy staff they comfort me. Thou preparest a table before me in the presence of mine enemies: thou anointest my head with oil; my cup runneth over. Surely goodness and mercy shall follow me all the days of my life: and I will dwell in the house of the LORD for ever. (Psalm 23)

∽ 28 ∾

A STORM-PROOF RELIGION

Matthew 8:23–27; Mark 4:35–41

And he arose, and rebuked the wind, and said unto the sea, Peace be still! And the wind ceased, and there was a great calm. (Mark 4:39)

We must have religion steeped in a faith which can withstand the stress of life's tribulations. We can build a storm-proof religion by having Jesus in our life, talking to the Lord through constant prayer and listening to Jesus' message. What I am talking about is a "storm-proof religion." We need a faith that is stress resistant, that is able to stand difficulty.

This pulpit is not interested in a gospel that works only inside these walls. I have called such a "hothouse faith." Such a plant can survive, and maybe thrive, as long as the temperature is kept moderate and constant. It cannot stand shifts in the temperature. That is no faith worth having. And, if our Christianity means nothing more to us than that, then we need to look for some other way or we need to look for THE WAY because we have not found it. Our faith needs to be able to stand stress.

I do not know how many people I have seen come into this church. At first, they seemed so enthusiastic, so exuberant, so eager, and they blossom so rapidly, flourish so much, are so active, and then in one way or another the temperature changes. They had a reverse in life. Some disappointment came to them. Things did not turn out as they thought they were going to turn out. And they wilted and collapsed. Or somebody said something to them, or they thought somebody said something about them. And they could not stand it. Or to use a figure of speech, a contrary wind capsized the boat. And what happened to them I do not know. They were last seen foundering and floundering, without anything to hold on to.

You can test your faith by whether or not it can stand stress when things do not go as you figured they would, when something happens that upsets your plans, when you have to alter your strategy, get a new game plan. If you collapse, your faith is lacking. I remember when the 747s first came out. I remember the apprehensiveness all of us had about these giant things. We read they were to hold three hundred people in one airplane. In order to allay the apprehensiveness of the flying public, the manufacturer of those huge things spread far and wide the word that they had had test pilots fly these things carrying more weight than they would ever carry in normal flight. They were tested under the most adverse conditions and found able to stand stress. When a plane was miraculously saved in Hawaii some time ago, the claim was that what went wrong was stress. Metal fatigue sheared the metal, cut it in two. The whole top of the thing went off.

We need a storm-proof religion.

Suppose I tell you today that I have come with the formula that will allow you to have religion that is storm-proof? There is no more wonderful word that I could ever speak to you than that we have a prescription for a religion that can stand stress, handle a storm, will not capsize, will not go under in heavy waters. That's what we need — religion that can stand stress and does not collapse and break up when things go wrong. That's what anybody needs who is going to live anytime at all in a world like this.

I want to follow an incident. It happens in the Gospel of Matthew in the eighth chapter. You'll find a companion passage in the Gospel of Mark in the fourth chapter. After having taught, the Lord says to his disciples, "Let us go over to the other side," for the command of life is to always keep moving. You cannot stand still — anybody's religion that is immobilized is soon paralyzed. If you are not growing in grace, you are calcifying in faith. To stand still is to go back. Oh, to be sure, there are moments and seasons in life when we cannot press forward as we did once, but to settle down at any level of Christian growth is to spoil the whole business.

A still church is a stagnant church. It does not have freshness moving through it. It does not have life. And the stillest thing you've ever seen is the thing you want least to be. Do you know what that is? Death is still, does not move, does not wrinkle any dresses, does not get any neckties askew. It is an awful stillness. The seven last words of many a church are these: "We never did it that way before."

The Lord Jesus says to his disciples, "Let us go over to the other side." The Lord is always calling his people forward. "Continue in my love," he says in the Gospel of John as he is about to depart. Don't quit. Keep moving. How we as Christians need to keep growing. There is so much we have not reached yet. God has worlds waiting on us, far more wonderful than anything we have experienced, if we will obey and keep going. "Follow me," he says. After he cured a man, he said, "You go. Don't stay here. Go back home. Tell your people what the Lord has done for you." Then, "Let us go over to the other side."

He was talking about the Sea of Galilee, which is an inland sea. Six or seven miles they had to travel across the Sea of Galilee. An inland sea can be as furious as, and perhaps more furious than, the open sea, because the open sea has such width to spread its turbulence. But an inland sea, like the Sea of Galilee, is confined, usually within mountains. I remember preaching in Central Africa years ago in Malawi. A man named Oliver Ransford has written about the most captivating thing in that section of old Central Africa: Lake Malawi. He described how it can change moods. He said that sometimes by day it is so calm, the lake is like a tilted mirror to catch the languid artistry of the sky — the reflection of the sky in the water. Then, he said, at evening, the mood of Lake Malawi changes; its color becomes a purple. And then by night, when it is calm and the moon is shining upon it, it is a thing of beauty, of gold. But it is located between two mountains, and sometimes the winds that gather back up in the hills come screaming and funneled, and then Lake Malawi is driven into an awful frenzy by the closeness of being limited by the walls of the mountains. The winds come with great fury, and the lake becomes an awful frothing thing, sometimes with waves fifteen feet high. Well, that is what Galilee is like.

It is an inland sea. There are mountains, and sometimes when the winds come screaming through, they meet in a concentrated fury, and they set that sea into an awful raging foam. You see, life gives us conditions, and we cannot tell what winds we are going to meet. They form somewhere back in the mountains, out of our view. And when they get to us, they are already formed, already at work, already rushing through. The only air we can control is by fans and electricity, but the great winds that come at us come from elsewhere.

That night the Sea of Galilee was at first calm and placid as they traveled the six or seven miles to the other side. Suddenly the winds came screaming down through the pass of the mountains. This sea, which had been so calm, became angry, frothing at the mouth, whitecapped waves billowing and dipping. The little ship was bouncing and tossing in the trough of the waves until the disciples were horrified. Now you must take notice of this. The people who were on that ship were not land lovers; they were seafaring people. They were fishermen. They knew the Sea of Galilee. They had fished on it. It was their profession, their business. But on that particular occasion, the fury of the storm was so great that it terrified them.

There was but one advantage which that frail craft, tossing upon this mad and angry sea, had — it had Jesus on board. That's the first element in this formula for a storm-proof religion: Jesus was on board. And if you are going to handle this business we call life, this voyage, this sea, you need the Lord on board. I tell you this day that I would not go out of these doors — in fact I would not want to stay inside here with all of you here — without the Lord on board. Who can tell what is going to happen? What threats, what dangers, are all around us?

You mean to tell me you are willing to walk these streets without the Lord?

You mean to tell me that you will get on these subways without the Lord?

You mean to tell me that you will contract a marriage without the Lord?

You meant to tell me that you will go into a hospital to be operated on and you don't have the Lord?

You mean to tell me that you will enter into a business transaction and you don't have Jesus at your side?

My God, what a fool you must be! You and I need the Lord on our side!

Young people, you need the Lord on board. The sea is treacherous and dangerous. It's filled not only with natural dangers but with many pirates that will rob your ship.

They had the Lord on board. There is no use in talking about anything else. There is no use in discussing how to win friends and influence people. There is no use in arguing with you about how to make your life successful. If you do not have this first ingredient in the formula — if you don't have the Lord — you can't make it right. If you have the Lord on board, you're in good condition.

When the storm got furious — the lightning flashing, the great thunder drums rolling, the wind screaming, and the waves thrashing — these experienced seamen were terrified. They made their living on the Sea of Galilee before they joined Jesus. But they had never seen a storm like this, and having him on board, they had sense enough to call him.

That's the second ingredient: when things happen in your life, you need enough presence of mind to call him. I do not know any other way to make this journey except to call on the Lord. There is no substitute for prayer. You and I can go over all the books on self-help and self-culture and how to improve our minds and vocabulary, but unless we learn the vocabulary of prayer, we are in a bad fix. I am not talking now about when only mild things happen. I'm talking about when great winds blow contrary in your life. You need to know how to call the Lord. Ask him to help you. Talk to him. Plead with him. Ask the Savior to help you. He is willing to heed you. He will carry you through. Be thankful for the privilege of asking him to protect your families and to take care of your children, to see about your hopes, to handle your needs, to correct your faults, to confirm your faith, to strengthen your determination, to give you the power to overcome, to stand the storm, to go on to see what the end will be. This is what we need.

We ought to talk regularly to the Lord about our needs. It ought not be a brier-covered path that we have to cross to get to the Lord. It ought to be a well-worn path so that we don't need a road map to find where the Lord is. We ought to travel that road so regularly that we can run hastily to meet him, tell him our trouble. When trouble is upon you, you don't have time to pick your way through thickets. You need right then to be able to talk with him, to ask him to help. You need, therefore, my brothers and sisters, to cultivate the prayer habit. I do not mean just an empty habit. I mean to cultivate constant regular practice of being before God in prayer. If you go to him when things are calm, you will find it easier in the storm to talk to him. You won't have to work your way through layers of difficulty, objections, qualifications, and uncertainties. If you've been talking with him, you can talk with him more easily when trouble comes.

That's the second ingredient. They called out, "Master, carest thou not that we perish?" The storm is raging. We are unable to handle it. These waves are mounting up. They are frothing at the mouth. A great and mighty tempest is blowing on this sea, and it looks like we are momentarily going down. It seems as if this ship cannot last any longer. "Master, carest thou not that we perish?"

They found the Lord asleep, but it was not the sleep of indifference. He was sleeping partly because he was weary but also because he knew what to do. Panic comes because of frustration. No one ever gets into a panic who knows what the next step is. We go to pieces because we don't know what to do next. There is no condition in life so bad if we know the next step. He knew what the next step was. He was asleep, and it was a sign of his identification with our humanity. I like that about our Lord. I am glad that he got tired and weary. When we are tired and weary, he knows what it is all about because he's traveled the road that we travel. He sweated our sweat, drank our water, ate our food, felt our loneliness, and suffered our sense of desertion. He knows all about our troubles. He's been this way, traveled this road. He knows all about your troubles.

> He knows where the road dips down.
> He knows where the currents are.
> He knows when the way is rough and rocky.
> He knows when it looks like your way is blocked and you cannot
>   make it another step.
> He knows what it is to feel weariness.

And so, he slept. He slept also because there was in our Lord a great and wondrous and mysterious and inexplicable combination of the divine and the human. He slept as a human. He got up as divine. And we see that over and over again in his life, that strange mixture of what was mortal and what was God himself. Have I ever told you how he wept at Lazarus's tomb? That was a man. But when he spoke, he spoke as God and said, "Lazarus come forth." It took a man to weep, but a god to speak. So he slept. They shook him and said, "Master, carest thou not that we perish?"

I can see him now as he shakes the cobwebs of slumber from his eyes, stretches, and stands up to see the sea. Matthew did not hear what he said. Matthew says that he looked out into the sea and rebuked it. I do not know if Matthew quite grasped what the Lord said, but the sea knew who was looking at it. Mark said that Jesus said something, and Mark heard what he said. He said, "Peace, be still." I do not think it was a loud voice. I don't think it had to be because the sea had heard that voice before, in the morning of creation when he said, "Let there be." So the sea was not unacquainted with the voice that it heard when he said, "Peace, be still." Dr. Goodspeed translates this into "Hush," like a mother talking to a child.

"Hush." The lightning folded its flame and ran back to its hiding place.

"Hush." The winds got still and fled to their homes in the hills.

"Hush." And the sea stretched out like a pet before its master.

"Hush." And the elements grew calm.

The Lord can speak peace to our souls. He says to us, "Hush, do not be disturbed. Do not be troubled. It is I — be not afraid. I will not let you fall. I will not let you go down. I will not let your enemy overtake you. I will not let trouble conquer you. I will not let sickness defeat you. I will not let enemies bring you into the dust. I will not let death defeat you. Hush, my child." Be still my soul. The Lord is on your side. Be still when the great storm clouds gather. Be still.

You've got the formula. One, keep the Lord on board. Two, do not mind calling him. And three, wait for him to answer. He may not be on your schedule, but he will not act late. He never fails. That is the one word that is not in his vocabulary. He will bless your life.

~ 29 ~

Struggling but Not Losing

2 Corinthians 4:8–10

We are troubled on every side, yet not distressed; we are perplexed, but not in despair; Persecuted, but not forsaken; cast down, but not destroyed; Always bearing about in the body the dying of the Lord Jesus, that the life also of Jesus might be made manifest in our body. (2 Corinthians 4:8–10)

You must not realize it, but you are out every day to find out what life is all about. Every person, whether the case is stated or left in silence, is trying to find out what this life is all about. We look for clues as to the nature of life; we search for some sign of a pattern; we believe that there is a design.

I heard my father long ago preach a sermon on "The Riddle of Life." In it he reflected upon what he called the "fascinating legend of the Sphinx at Thebes." In that legend the creature with a lion's body and a human head terrorized the people of the city of Thebes by demanding the answer to a riddle taught her by the muses. Each time the riddle was answered incorrectly, the cruel Sphinx would devour a human soul. At last, Oedipus gave the correct answer. He was throned by a grateful citizenry, and the Sphinx thereupon killed herself. So the riddle was answered in an old and fascinating legend, but in some way or another in the days of our years the riddle is put to us in the events of our existence. What is life all about? What is its nature? Does it have a pattern? Can you solve its riddle? Are you able to see a design, a meaning?

You will misread it if you decide that life is a picnic, a frolic, or a party. It has carefree hours, but they are the exception. Life is a struggle; that is what it is, a struggle from the day we are born until the day we die. Children are barely born, and right where life begins there is a struggle between life and death. How

182

is the baby? How is the mother? are the questions we ask, and in so saying we recognize that there has been a struggle. The infant struggles to walk. Would you like to know, by the way, what the riddle was the Sphinx at the city of Thebes asked of its citizens? It was this, "What is it that has one voice and yet becomes four-footed and then two-footed and then three-footed?" It is, of course, a human being with a single voice who first struggles to crawl on all fours, then, as a baby, struggles to walk on two feet, and then struggles at last to stay upright by leaning on a cane.

You and I will never understand what this life is all about until we see it as a struggle. This struggle is all tied up with our capacity to suffer. Frederick Robertson, the English preacher of the mid-1800s, often described our human plight and perhaps his own short and tortured life. He said, and some of you will say it is all too gloomy and melancholy a reading of life, that our universal heritage is woe: "Men of poverty we are not all, men of weak ability we are not all — but the man not of sorrows is as yet unborn." And I may add, his mother has already died.

All that is about us is subject to injury, which opens the way for struggle. The skin of the human frame can be broken, bringing forth blood. There runs beneath the skin, crossed and crisscrossed in layers unbelievable, a network of nerves, every fiber, every inch, every scintilla of which may become the home of pain, and so easily. There is no gap in all of those nerves into which the finest needle may be thrust without producing pain. In a sense, which the psalmist hardly meant, we are fearfully made.

The mental machinery, Robertson continued, is even more sensitive. The inner mind is more exposed to shock and wounds than the outer skin, and the sensitive network which comprises the mind is a thousand times more alive to agony than the physical nerves that quiver and ache when they are cut. There is such a thing as disappointment in this world, and we all taste it sometimes. There is such a thing as affection rejected and hurled back on itself. There is such a thing as slight, insult, scorn, and sarcasm, which cut the spirit and then rub salt in the wound. There is such a thing as sickness, sin, and sorrow. Robertson, himself so troubled, seemed to be describing himself.

Could I but mention another aspect of our being which makes us liable to suffering and struggle? We are creatures made to love, to give our hearts in trust and surrender one to the other. This is as natural with us as breathing. Withholding love and trust are unnatural impulses. This capacity for love opens us to so many hurts and to so much struggle, bitter, anguished, raw, bleeding suffering. The moment you give your trust in friendship or love, you open yourself, expose yourself to betrayal and humiliation. This is the theme of so much that is most touching in music, poetry, and theater. Have you not seen such love and trust rejected and trampled upon? Is there anyone who has not passed through this or who is not passing through it now? I have wept inwardly with so many young women who have been abandoned at a fearful time and whose sad word was, "I trusted him." I have listened to scores of men who have said, "I tried to give her everything, and now this!" I will not peer down the street where parents lament the indifference of their children and whose wail is fashioned out of their love.

So we get hurt, run risks, and must struggle day by day, for life is a fight! And if you are not careful, it is a losing fight! The struggle can leave one numb, cold, bitter, and cursing, off in a corner — sobbing, on some skid row looking for peace in the bottom of a bottle or somewhere else shooting poison into the veins, trying to drive sorrow and struggle away.

There is an antidote for this plight, true and tried. Hear, if you will, this Scripture all laden and heavy with suffering, struggling, and something else or, better still, somebody else who makes all of the difference. This is one man's litany of suffering and struggle. "We are troubled on every side,... are perplexed.... Persecuted,... cast down." It is a Christian man, Paul, talking — the world's best-known proponent and promoter of the gospel of Jesus Christ. When will fools stop talking about the faith of Christ as something soft and innocent as to what life's hurts are all about?

You are a Christian. You don't know what the world is like? I
have known very, very few Christian people who have not known
intimately how ugly and brutal life can be. Our faith is not a
hothouse faith, off somewhere in a never-never land of innocent
contemplation. The church of Jesus Christ was not born in a quiet
ivory tower of isolated, insulated, and protected reflection. It was
born in bloodshed and brutality, amidst nails, spears, hammers,
lies, curses, gambling, and dark betrayal. The church came to be
not by serene meditation alone, but it was jostled and pushed by
the mystery religions of Egypt and Asia Minor, the hard-nosed,
relentless logic of Greek philosophy, the harsh legalism and en-
mity of those who would not see and would not believe, and
the brutal cruelty of the most ruthless empire the world has ever
known: Rome.

The man who wrote our text knew what it's all about. You
know, the biggest fools are those who think that all which they
think is smart got started when they were born. "Mom and Dad,
you don't know what it's all about." How vain and foolish can
youth be! Some do not realize that there is no mom or dad who
was not once their age. All of these smart operators on their way
to jail in government think they started it all. Check the encyclopedia, and you will see that about 1100 B.C. investigations
revealed large-scale plunder and corruption in high places, strikes,
and power grabbing in the city of Thebes.

The man who wrote the words I have quoted was no shielded,
insulated child of privilege. As a young man, he watched and supported the death of Deacon Stephen by stoning. Think of rocks
and stones being hurled at a human body until bones are crushed
and life is literally knocked out of the frame. You are onto something more brutal than stabbing or shooting. Here was a man
talking out of twenty-five or more years campaigning up and
down the empire, sailing, walking, and riding. Look at the labels on his baggage! Tarsus, Damascus, Antioch — all for Jesus.
Look again at this lonely pilgrim for Jesus, preaching, arguing,
defending, and explaining the gospel in many strange and hos-
tile forums: no family, many enemies, suspicion, attacks, jailings,

and desertions. Look again at the labels on his baggage: Lystra, Derbe, Iconium, Perga, Ephesus, Corinth, Athens, Thessalonica, Philippi — twenty-five years alone, traveling, talking, and working. He knew the unreliability of friends. He was so sick one night, maybe in Troas, that they sent for the doctor whose name, maybe, was Luke. Cold-shouldered by a church he planted and loved, talked about unkindly by people to whom he taught Jesus and whom he baptized, I think he qualifies in the University of Hard Knocks.

Now listen to how Paul talked about suffering and struggling but not losing. The difference between winning and losing in his life was Jesus Christ. It was the gospel which put joy bells ringing in his heart and singing in his soul, the love of Jesus which shed abroad bright sunshine in his spirit. "We have this treasure in earthen vessels" — Paul was saying that he was not much, but he had a great possession. He was very weak, but he had a friend who was very strong. "We have this treasure in earthen vessels. . . . We are troubled on every side" — all around there is a hard struggle — "troubled on every side, yet not distressed; we are perplexed," puzzled, confused, sometimes, "but not in despair; persecuted, but not forsaken; cast down, but not destroyed," struggling but not losing.

There is no place for defeat in God's plan. I used to hear my father say, and God knows I have found this true, that Christians are like rubber balls. The harder you throw them down, the higher they bounce. We may be sure that we shall overcome! "Thanks be to God, which giveth us the victory through our Lord Jesus Christ" (1 Corinthians 15:57). "For whatsoever is born of God overcometh the world: and this is the victory that overcometh the world, even our faith" (1 John 5:4). In Jesus we shall triumph over every foe, overcome every malady, every pain, and every sorrow. In 1952 the Concord Church structure covering a city block was consumed by fire. The first sermon in the new and larger edifice was taken from Psalm 126: "They that sow in tears shall reap in joy. He that goeth forth and weepeth, bearing precious seed, shall doubtless come again with rejoicing, bringing his sheaves with him" (vv. 5–6). Every Christian can be confident of such outcome.

God is going to win, and we who enlist in his army are going to win because we are his, and he is ours. When our warfare is over, we shall claim the triumph, and we shall go stately stepping to the great coronation, waving palms of victory in our hands and shouting, "We have overcome the wicked one." We shall march on through floods and flames, through sufferings and sorrows, until the great victory banquet of the Lamb. We shall come up from every side, from the north, south, east, and west carrying our crosses, bearing our burdens, weeping our tears, suffering our sorrows, limping with our hurts, and nursing our wounds. When the journey is past, we shall live, love, learn, and labor in that sunlit land where the flowers never fade, the day never dies, and the song never stills.

∽ 30 ∾

THREE DAYS THAT CHANGED THE WORLD

1 Corinthians 15:3–4

> For I delivered unto you first of all that which I also received, how that Christ died for our sins according to the scriptures; And that he was buried, and that he rose again the third day according to the scriptures. (1 Corinthians 15:3–4)

I want to preach what you might call a post-Easter Sunday sermon, and there are several reasons why I want to talk about this. In February of 1856, Charles Haddon Spurgeon on a Sunday morning in the New Park Street Church, whose congregation would later worship in the Metropolitan Tabernacle and where he would have a preaching ministry as far as hearers were concerned unrivaled by any pastor in the English-speaking world, began that sermon by saying that he had been examining why so many churches were so staid and so chilled. And he said he tracked the apostolic preaching back to its source to find out what the difference was. It was not just in the fact that there was a different type of oratory inherited from the Greek orators which later Christian preachers adopted, nor was it to be found in the fact that the New Testament preacher followed the laws of rhetoric. He went on to say, nor was it that they did not take texts, though I am not sure about Spurgeon on that because at Pentecost Peter did take a text. He said from the book of Joel, "I will pour out my spirit upon all flesh." But Spurgeon said that day, the reason why the apostolic preaching set the world on fire was that the New Testament preachers always preached the Resurrection.

At Pentecost it was Peter's assertion that "you crucified him and God raised him from the dead." And when they went up to the temple, Peter and John, in the aftermath of their healing of the lame man, said that the man's healing was not an inexplicable marvel but a derivative miracle, for God had raised Jesus from the dead. That was the central miracle. "It was the preaching of the Resurrection," said Spurgeon, "that first aroused the ire of the Council and hailed the apostles before them for a hearing." And as soon as they got out, it was the preaching of the Resurrection that they uttered.

If you follow the apostolic preaching, the people brought their gifts, there in the fourth chapter of Acts, because they preached the Resurrection. I am convinced that it is one of the chief achievements of Satan that we preach the Resurrection only on Easter Sunday, for here is the central truth of the Christian faith. Here is what supremely sets it apart.

When R. W. Dale was at Carrs Lane Church in Birmingham, England, successor to John Angel James, on a Saturday before Easter, he was reading the account of the Resurrection, and it came upon him with a fresh force that Christ is actually alive. He said I must tell my people, "Christ lives!" And after that, never a Sunday came in Carrs Lane Church but that an Easter anthem was sung in that congregation.

So I want to talk this evening about "Three Days That Changed the World." Let me read the passage from the start of the fifteenth chapter of Paul's first letter to the Corinthians: "For I delivered unto you first of all that which I also received, how that Christ died for our sins according to the scriptures; And that he was buried, and that he rose again the third day according to the scriptures."

There are days, though they may be the flash point of a long-smoldering circumstance, that alter the world. If you are ever a tourist, or if you have been a tourist in Quebec, upstate from New York, they will point out Fort Ticonderoga, where the French general Louis Montcalm successfully defended the fort. When you go to Quebec, they will carry you to the Plains of Abraham, the sight of the battle between the English general James Wolfe and the French general Louis Montcalm. It is generally felt among historians that if the British general had not prevailed on the battlefield on the Plains of Abraham on that day in September 1759, the

French influence on this continent would very likely have con-
tinued, and this sermon might well be in French. That day in
September 1759 altered the course of the language on the North
American continent. Come closer to home. If in April 1846 Santa
Anna's army at San Jacinto had prevailed on that day, this sermon
might well be in Spanish.

For there are days that alter the course of things. One day di-
vides the student from the graduate, the pupil from the alumnus,
and how many countless bridegrooms I have seen perspiring, no,
sweating, because they knew the momentous hour grew near that
for better or worse would alter their lives forever. We Christian
people have three days that altered the world, that shook the
world from center to circumference, and will affect events until
time falls exhausted at the feet of eternity — three days that altered the direction of history, arrested the drift of time, and turned
around the sequence of occurrence. Three days!

The first day — Friday. A hill shaped like a skull, an execution, a corpse, a tomb. What did it all mean? Some of the noblest
minds of these two millennia have wrestled with the meaning of
that first day: Irenaeus and Origen, Augustine, Anselm and Aqui-
nas, Barth and Tillich, and Luther. What did it mean? And these
have many theories as to what that first day means. There is the
legal theory that a law had been violated. A sentence was im-
posed, and on that cross Christ accepted in himself the penalty.
Then five hundred years ago Hugo Grotius, the Dutch theolo-
gian, propounded the theory that Calvary meant wiping away an
embarrassment in God's governance of the universe, in removing
an awful shame that a violation had occurred and had not been
righted. Then of course, there is the moral doctrine of what happened on that first day — that Christ showed in his exemplary
way how far God would go to save his people. And there is the
revelatory doctrine that God revealed the heartbeat of his love at
Calvary and at the same time unmasked the powers of evil, took
away from them their pretense of respectability, pulled off from
them their cloak of honor, and showed them to be a wicked government in alliance with a blasphemous religion turned against

the fairest the world has ever seen. For the cross forever reveals the wickedness of men, and we see over and over again conniving political operators joining hands with prostituted religionists to crucify the best the world has ever seen.

When that day had wrought its way, it was shown that Joseph Caiaphas, with all of his gold plates on embroidered linen, stood on the side of hell. It ought to be a message to us with our gaudy capes and poor women dressed as nurses hovering over us and fluttering with aspirin tablets and orange juice.

Well, all of these theories may well have truth in them, but not one of them tells me everything about that first day, nor can all of them together tell me what happened. As a boy I could not read the account of our Lord's death without tears coming to my eyes, and I still cannot. For I know in some way I have never been able to explain that he took a lick that was meant for me. I know that where our slates were all blotched and marred, he wiped them clean. And I know that he got under a load that I was meant to carry and that where the charges stood against me, he cleared them. If in Eden I see a tree forbidden, at Calvary I see a tree forgiving. If in Eden I see a tree prohibited, at Calvary I see a tree provided. But in some way deeper than I can ever say, he made it all right with my soul. He manumitted the slave's bondage, brought the exile back to his native land, put the orphan at the father's table, and called him or her a child, an heir. I know that at Calvary that first day, my condition was forever altered and changed, and I am now a child of the royal house.

> Was it for crimes that I have done He groaned upon the tree?
> Amazing pity! grace unknown! And love beyond degree!
> Well might the sun in darkness hide And shut his glories in,
> When Christ, the might Maker, died For man, the creature's sin.

The first day.

Concerning the second day, the Scriptures do not speak much. The third chapter of 1 Peter at verse 19 says, "He was freed in the spirit and went and preached to spirits in prison." Now, I am not under any warrant to preach any second probation, the doctrine that gave rise to the whole Roman Catholic doctrine of purgatory.

Those of us who have lost kin who did not accept Christ feel sometimes a strange sadness, for I am among those. And I do not know the meaning of this cryptic passage that he went and preached to the spirits in prison, nor do I have warrant to preach a second probation.

But I do read again that word our Lord spoke about a shepherd. Was he talking about himself? Is he the one who left the ninety and nine and went searching for one lost sheep who had strayed, beguiled by some tempting tuft of grass or led on by some inviting waterfall? Until...I do not know how long *until* is, and I have no warrant to preach a second probation, and I shall not. But until...not until darkness falls. But until...not until the chill of evening comes. But until...not until briers cut the Shepherd's hands. But until...not until thorns cut and lacerate the feet. But until....Until...I do not know how long *until* is. I do not know what he preached. Did he take that text from the old book, "Arise, shine for thy light has come"? I do not know. Or did he utter again the words he spoke when he addressed himself to the deepest places of Lazarus's death and said, "I am the resurrection and life"? I do not know. But he preached to the spirits chained in darkness. In vain, I do not know. I leave the second day.

The third day should be in all our preaching all of the time — all of the time. Ah, my brother, you have no better word to preach than that third day. It belongs not to one Sunday of the year; it belongs to the kerygma of the Christian proclaimer always — the third day.

In the imagination of the mind I seem to see the night beginning to disappear. Morning begins to draw a thin pencil of light across the eastern sky. The moon begins to leave the sky, the queen of the night, to make way for the king of the day to rise. The sky begins to blush shyly at the love song of the dawning as morning comes.

The strong Son of God shakes himself. That grave which held Adam strains under his movements. That grave which somewhere in the lonely lost summit of Nebo held Moses begins to shiver. That grave from which Abraham could not be extricated begins to tremble. That grave which the lyrical poetry of Isaiah could not move begins to tremble. That grave which was not charmed by the music of David begins to tremble. Look at him! Look at him! The strong Son of God lays aside those garments dipped in blood, clothes himself in the glory of the apparel of his lordship, steps forth in the morning light, and declares, "I am he that was dead; behold, I am alive forevermore. I've got the keys of hell and death." Christ lives!

And of course we ought not merely repeat that in any parabolic fashion. We ought to apply it to every circumstance of life. Christ lives! As you travel along Stemmons Freeway here in Dallas, Christ lives! Women preparing their dinner, Christ lives! Men going to their offices, Christ lives!

I have just come through a great teaching and testing time, as many of you have. I have passed through surgery and have come out of it surer of one thing than ever before — Christ lives, lives in me! Christ lives! I do not know how long I have now, but as long as I am to preach the gospel, every time I preach it, in one way or another I shall declare, Christ lives!

Let every tyrant pressing his heels upon the necks of the oppressed know, Christ lives! Let every faker in every high political office, wherever it is, know Christ lives! Christ lives! If thousands are still to hear my voice, please God! I shall declare to them, Christ lives! But if I am to be in some humble and rustic chapel, preaching to some simple people in some backwater of the land, I shall say to them, Christ lives!

When time hoarsens this voice and whatever ring there may be in it, I shall whisper, however throatily, Christ lives! When I come down to the slippery shores of Jordan, I have but one crossing password, Christ lives! I shall pass through its swelling current with those words upon my heart, Christ lives! When I stand on the shores of everlasting deliverance, I shall repeat those words, Christ lives! My spirit will sweep through the celestial plains, and I will cry again, Christ lives! When the gates of new life open to me, I will shout again, Christ lives! As I go stately stepping up the broad avenues of the glory land, I shall salute angels and archangels, prophets, priests, and kings, with the glorious words, Christ lives! When I kneel down at the lily-white throne and look at his nail-pierced feet, surrender my commission and thank him that he made me a preacher — a preacher down here — I shall cry once more, Christ lives!

ᵕ᷂ 31 ᷈ᵕ

THREE WOMEN AND GOD

The Book of Ruth

And she said, Behold, thy sister-in-law is gone back unto her people, and unto her gods: return thou after thy sister-in-law. And Ruth said, Entreat me not to leave thee, or to return from following after thee: for whither thou goest, I will go, and where thou lodgest, I will lodge, thy people shall be my people, and thy God my God. (Ruth 1:15–16)

We almost always preach about men. A great deal is lost, I think, when we overlook a full half of the human family. And so, now, I want to preach about some women. I wanted to call this "A Family Love Story," but that does not quite say what I wish to say. And so I will call it "Three Women and God."

The book of Ruth is an intriguing book, sometimes said to have been written to establish a certain ethnic openness among the people of Israel. But it is also an endlessly engaging book. I always put the little blue thread right at the book of Ruth because I can never find it. It is set so early in the Old Testament that I am always looking somewhere else for it. The word *God* is mentioned very little in this book, and yet it is one of the noble expositions on what seminary people like to call "theodicy" — the ways of God with humankind.

It is the account of a family: Elimelech, his wife, Naomi, and their two sons, Chilion and Mahlon. They migrate from Israel because hard times have come upon that land. They travel east of the Jordan to Moab, whose purple hills form at evening an almost somber background to the long, strange history of ancient Israel. They have gone to Moab seeking a better life. All of us who are children of migrant communities might well ponder what must

Preached at Princeton Theological Seminary in Princeton, New Jersey, for theological students and pastors. — GCT have gone through the minds of this man, his wife, and their two sons. We might especially wonder about the father and mother who are giving up familiar surroundings and are about to make their way, to establish their home, in a strange land. It is likely they knew very few people in this land, where they would be looked upon as foreigners among people whose customs were not familiar to them.

Some competent person ought to set down in a skillful way the account of our black migrations in America and the raw, ugly circumstances that prompted the migrations of blacks from the South, northward and westward. These were a people driven by circumstances. How great must have been the anxiety they felt as they sat for the last time by the lamplight of their humble southern quarters. These people were determined that their children would have better opportunity than they had and were willing to brave the hazards and the uncertainties of a strange and distant part of the nation.

When one looks back upon Naomi and her husband, Elimelech, and their sons, one hears a replica of what many of us have gone through. This was the pattern of migration for this family. They establish a home. They make a life; and in the natural course of time, the husband dies. These sons take wives to themselves. It is an interesting thing to see romances take place, develop, blossom, and flower. These lads, Mahlon and Chilion, marry Moabite girls, lovely in their lithe, highland beauty. And for ten years, the two generations — this widowed mother-in-law and mother, these daughters-in-law, and these two sons — all live together. But after a while, something occurs — and those of us who preach ought to never forget that there lingers ever over human life an "after a while" — the sons die. Life is rarely one thing or the other. It is almost always a mixture of joy and sorrow, of gladness and grief, of sunshine and shadows, of sickness and health, of life and death. This is life, and preaching ought never be far away from tears and laughter. Any preaching that is going to search the hearts of people must search them at the depths of their gladness and at those profound moments of their grief. These sons die because the generations rise and the generations pass away.

Now Naomi is left widowed. As she plans to return to her
native land, she says to her two daughters-in-law, with a wonderfully mature beauty and character, "I have no other sons for you,
and if I, barren as I am in my old age, could bear children, you
could not wait for them. Go back to your own people." What
unselfishness on her part. Some have suggested that maybe this
ought to be called the book of Naomi. There is a sense in which
it is she who is the heroine. She is willing to undertake whatever
uncertainties and hazards are involved in returning to her land
minus her sons and her daughters-in-law. "Go back," she says.
"Go back to your own people."

They kiss. It is one of the unforgettable farewell scenes of Scripture. The widowed Naomi, now bereft of her sons, starts back
toward the land of Israel, having heard that circumstances have
altered back at home. She says to her daughters-in-law, "Go back
to your own people."

Orpah goes a few steps, kisses her mother-in-law, and turns
back toward the hill country of Moab from which she has come.
Perhaps Orpah finds happiness. Perhaps she marries again, for
there is no beauty quite like that of a woman already attractive,
who has known sorrow early in her years. And so very likely Orpah finds a new life, but for us she disappears forever. She has
come very close to salvation history. One need not blame her; it is
a natural impulse for her to go back home. But there is a certain
sadness, a wee bit of melancholy, that settles upon us when we
realize that here is a woman who touches so close to the whole
lineage of God's revelation to people and turns away from it and
disappears in the purple hills of Moab. How sad it is for anybody
to miss life, but how doubly tragic it is for any person to come
close to the meaning of life, to its richness, to its fullness, to its
grandeur, to its glory, and to then turn away from it.

I spoke at Southern University and spent a day or two among
the gentle people of my upbringing. I saw people there, hundreds
of them, who have actually made it to places of great responsi-
bility — people who came along with me who could not even go
into a public library at one time. They have overcome in spite of

almost impossible odds. But how tragic that a land like America, so blessed, so great, would have dealt so cruelly with some of its children. And how sad that the heirs of people who braved so much and dared so much and who came out of the dark night of slavery with a bright vision of who they were and what they might become should be succeeded in our day by so many who seem to have lost all sense of direction and purpose. Are the heirs of such courage to waste it all in aimlessness?

I weep for the black American community when I remember whose descendants we are. I was born fifty years after slavery, or thereabouts. I've eaten in former slave quarters and preached in former slave churches, and I knew people who came out of that dark night. I knew their determination. I knew their courage; I knew their willingness to sacrifice. In 1854, the *Richmond Monitor,* then the leading paper of the city of Richmond, which would shortly be the capital of the Confederacy, printed an editorial that said, "The Negro is here and is here forever. And he is ours and he is ours forever." In 1854, from the slave quarters of the South, there came a reply, not in the print of the *Richmond Monitor* but rising out of heartbreak and hope, "I'm so glad trouble don't last always." How sad that we who are the heirs of that tradition should come now to a place where we do not know what is the next step we ought to take.

As the nation has chosen to turn away from its democratic vision by its choice of racism and sexism, so have we in our churches chosen to distort the vision of the kingdom of God by limiting the full exercise of the gifts of women. We have excluded women from the pulpit and other areas of church leadership and dared to claim that this is God's will. We are guilty of an unholy liaison between sexism and the privilege of power. This is not of God. There is in Christ neither Jew nor Greek, neither bond nor free, neither male nor female.

Ruth, with some deep interior motive of love and duty and regard for her elder, would not turn back. She speaks those tender words which are among the most moving words, be they between boy and girl or between parent and child, in any literature in any part of the world. "Entreat me not," she said, "to leave thee, or to return from following after thee: for whither thou goest, I will go; and where thou lodgest, I will lodge ... and thy God [will be] my God" (Ruth 1:16). Had she seen this elderly woman in prayer? Had she seen this woman's sterling faith under difficult circumstances? Had she found in her mother-in-law a role model? "Thy God will be my God." And let me say to you quite honestly, the strongest preaching that you will ever do will be in what you are. If you have principles and decency and purpose and a determination not to exploit your people, there will be people who will look to you and glorify the God of heaven. The God of heaven will honor your ministry far beyond what you will be able to scramble and scrounge and plot and scheme to receive. God will do it.

And so Ruth follows her mother-in-law. Boaz sees her and sees in her beauty deepened by sorrow. Believe me, you're not ready to preach the gospel at its depths and heights until something has cut you. People can see a difference in those who have experienced pain. They can tell when someone has not yet had that experience, too, as in the case of a young woman singing in a concert hall. A man in the audience said to another, "There is something wrong with her voice." The other said, "No, there is not anything wrong with her voice; it is her soul. She has not been hurt yet." And some day, something will cross your life that will bring you to tears and heartbreak, but it will be the means by which you gain access to other people's hearts. And so Ruth enters the lineage of the household of faith.

When I turn to the fifth verse of that first chapter of the book of Matthew, there her name stands. She becomes the mother of Obed, Obed becomes the father of Jesse, Jesse becomes the father of David, and of that lineage comes the Savior of the world. This Moabite girl, this alien child of the hills, this foreigner, this woman in a society that devalued and oppressed women, by loyalty to love and to duty enters the covenant of grace. And her name stands there and will stand there as long as the stars shine and as long as the ocean moves, because she found that which is the most precious thing in the world, an association with the covenant of grace in the household of faith.

Who could have imagined that God would choose to use a humble foreign woman in such a way? God's ways are not our ways. Yet some of us are trying even now to choose for God who should preach and who should not. Some have boldly declared, "God cannot call a woman to preach." How arrogant! How outrageous! The call by God to proclaim this gospel of light and life is completely in God's hands. It is a divine prerogative and only a divine prerogative. It is to our shame that we would miss the glorious gospel of Jesus Christ because we prefer our prejudices over God's choice of servants. We misrepresent our Lord and dishonor his name. Our Christ is infinitely to be preferred over our prejudices of gender or race.

Let me conclude with a personal word to you who prepare for ministry. Years ago, I preached in a southern city where George Beverly Shea, the song leader for Dr. Billy Graham, was on the program that night. He told a story from his own youth, about his involvement in Wall Street finance, for which he had a real talent. It caused him to show up later and later for customary family dinner and the gathering around the piano, as some of us did in the long ago, to sing the hymns of faith. His mother must have sensed that something was happening to him internally, so she left a note for him to come early from work the next day and to play a piece on the piano while the other family members were arriving for dinner. He said that she had left that simple, old, truly evangelical hymn,

> I'd rather have Jesus than silver or gold,
> I'd rather be His than have riches untold;
> I'd rather have Jesus than houses or lands,
> I'd rather be led by His nail-pierced hand.
>
> I'd rather have Jesus than men's applause,
> I'd rather be faithful to His dear cause;
> I'd rather have Jesus than worldwide fame,
> I'd rather be true to His holy name.*

I'd Rather Have Jesus by Rhea F. Miller and George Beverly Shea. Copyright 1922 and 1939; copyright renewed 1950 and 1966 by Chancel Music. Assigned

I want to say to you something that I do not often say. I have come now to the evening of my life. It has been a wonderful day. I never dreamed, having been born when I was and where I was, ninety miles from where land runs out in the deepest South, that such wide opportunities should have opened to me. However, let me say this to you from my heart, my young friends. The faith that I now have, I have not won in any bucolic cloistered surrounding. I have won my faith in the toughest arena in the world, in the thrust and counter-thrust of public life in the city of New York. I've known people of great wealth, but I'd rather have Jesus than silver or gold; I'd rather have Jesus than riches untold. I have heard great auditoriums echo with acclaim from one end of the earth to the other. You name it—New York, Cleveland, Chicago, London, Tokyo, Miami—but I'd rather have Jesus than people's applause.

I have known great people — Malcolm and Martin. Once, preaching in Old First Church here in Princeton about twenty-five years ago, I spent a morning with Albert Einstein. But I'd rather hear the gospel of Jesus Christ than all of the wisdom of scientific genius. No matter how famous or obscure the preacher, no matter whether highly educated or prayerfully self-taught, no matter whether male or female, I'd rather hear from him or her the riches of the pure and simple gospel than all of the astonishing insights of science. I'd rather have Jesus; I'd rather have Jesus than anything this world affords. I'd rather have Jesus.

✑ 32 ✑

WHAT "BORN AGAIN" REALLY MEANS

John 3:3

Jesus answered and said unto him, Verily, verily, I say unto thee, Except a man be born again, he cannot see the kingdom of God. (John 3:3)

How the term "born again" is bandied about these days. How widely and wildly it is used. Maybe we ought to begin by taking the method of the Eastern Orthodox theologians. They reason toward the being of God by what they call the *via negativa,* the way of the negatives, in other words, by saying what it is not. As for "born again," what does it not mean?

"Born again" does not mean a way of praising some officeholder every week; it does not mean that. "Born again" does not mean political philosophy for fighting some *ism* or another; it does not mean that. "Born again" does not mean a hustle for getting money; it does not mean that. "Born again" does not mean support for apartheid; it does not mean that. "Born again" does not mean meanness with everybody who does not agree with you; it does not mean that. That's not born again; that's a lie. "Born again" does not mean being a crank; it does not mean that. "Born again" does not mean racism — from pulpit or via television. It does not mean that.

Now I'll go on to what it does mean. The term is mentioned twice in the New Testament. Once in the twenty-third verse of the first chapter of the first letter of Peter. "Born again," he says, "not of corruptible seed, but of incorruptible, by the word of God, which liveth and abideth for ever." The other time where the term "born again" appears in the New Testament in the exact form occurred one night when Jesus talked with a man:

There was a man of the Pharisees, named Nicodemus, a ruler of the Jews: The same came to Jesus by night, and said unto him,

Rabbi, we know that...no man can do these miracles that thou doest, except God be with him. Jesus answered and said unto him, Verily, verily, I say unto thee, Except a man be born again, he cannot see the kingdom of God.

How those of us who preach and teach have made much of the fact that Nicodemus came by night to see Jesus. Was it that being one of those ruling elders of Israel, a person of many affairs, that he had to finish his day's work, clear his desk, and by the time he did that, night had come? At any rate, Nicodemus went to see Jesus; the Scripture says that he came to Jesus by night. Many of the great scenes of the Bible occurred at night. We've gone through some of them here the last few months. Nicodemus came by night. It may have been that the thronging crowds and their clamor for an audience, pleadings that jostled constantly around our Lord by day, gave no opportunity for someone to engage in the kind of conversation that Nicodemus desired to have with Jesus. And so he came when the crowds had gone, by night.

I said that many scenes of the Bible are set at night. But never was there a conversation more far-reaching for all succeeding generations of believers than this conversation with Nicodemus and Jesus held in the nighttime. It may have been that Nicodemus came by night because he was embarrassed, being the person he was, enjoying the position he held, having the reputation which belonged to him. Coming to talk with a wandering preacher from Galilee may have been embarrassing to Nicodemus. Did you know that there are people who are embarrassed about seeking any information or interest about the Lord? I had a professional man in this city say to me once that he felt uncomfortable in church because he was used to being in charge wherever he was. In charge! Poor dying man, in charge! Here we are borne by every wind that comes along, reacting to every sunrise. In charge! Soon to be carted out.... Well, that's a little cruel; let me make it nicer, to be hauled out. In charge! In charge! In charge! We will take an interest and openly and eagerly ask information about everything else. We want to know how to repair our cars, how to insulate our houses, how to cook cornbread, how to get from one place to the other, but how limited and reserved and sensitive so many of us become when it turns to a matter about seeking to know the Lord better — how to live lives that will be well pleasing in God's sight.

It may be that Nicodemus was embarrassed. Do I talk to someone now who would be embarrassed to ask anything of anybody about the Lord? Embarrassed to have any conversation about the Lord's goodness? Embarrassed?

Of course, was there ever so great a contrast between people as the one between Nicodemus and Jesus? Looking at it, you know, by our ugly judgment, here was Nicodemus, a ruler, a member of the Sanhedrin council, one of only seventy of all the people of Israel who had to do with determining the direction and making judgments and decisions about the nation. Nicodemus, a ruler; Jesus with no credentials, except what he himself declared, "The spirit of the Lord is upon me, for he has anointed me." Nicodemus, well placed; Jesus with no place to lay his head. Nicodemus, a man of wealth and, doubtless, of influence, wealth because he could afford to supply the expensive spices for Jesus' burial. Jesus had nothing except the cloak that he wore. Here they are together; what a contrast. Nicodemus, master in Israel; Jesus, a wandering preacher from Galilee. You remember the lines of Kipling,

> Oh, East is East, and West is West, and never the twain shall meet,
> . . . .
> But there is neither East nor West, Border, nor Breed, nor Birth,
> When two strong men stand face to face, though they come from
>   the ends of the earth.

What we have here is not really two strong men. We have one man with a great need coming to another who has it in his power, who has in his hands the power, to meet the first man's needs. It is not an equal meeting. This is a suppliant come to a supplier. This is an asker come to a giver. And immediately Nicodemus starts off wrong: "Master, rabbi, we know that thou art a teacher come from God." But what Nicodemus needed was not a teacher; he needed a Savior.

It is a wrong notion, believe me, to say "To know is to do." As a matter of fact, that word *education* comes from the Latin word *educere,* which means "to lead forth" or "to lead out." What we need is somebody to lead us out; that is the ultimate education. We do not need more facts; we need somebody who will lead us out, somebody we can trust, somebody we can depend upon, somebody who will not mislead us.

So Nicodemus needed a Savior, not a teacher. He already knew more than enough. He was a master in Israel; he knew the Law of Moses; he knew the Decalogue; he knew the Prophets. He was a master in Israel, a scholar, a governor. He did not need a teacher; he needed a Savior. You do not primarily need somebody telling you what to do. Oh, we may be able to stand that, but we need more greatly somebody to tell us *how* we're going to do what we ought to do. Our conscience will tell us what we need to do, but our conscience does not tell us how to do it. That is where a Savior comes in. Empowerment is our need!

A study from the University of Chicago predicts that by the year 2000, if we continue at the rate we're going, 70 percent of black children will be born to unwed mothers. You can't make a race like that. Only 30 percent of black males will be employed by the year 2000. I don't have to worry too much about the year 2000, but some of you had better think about where you're going to be in the year 2000. I'm talking about the wiping out of a race. I'm talking about a whole race practically on public dole. I'm talking about a whole race without any moral fiber, without any faith, without any strength, wandering in a wilderness, in a morass of ignorance and helplessness; you had better come back to God. We need a Savior. Empowerment!

All of us were dazed and shocked. Seeing the *Challenger* suddenly explode in midair, that awful tragedy left us all shaken. In death, those brave astronauts left us an example. They were what America was meant to be — black and white and Asian, male and female. There are many lessons to be learned. One, of course, is that we are creatures and in all of our proud achievements, we must be humble.

Tom Wicker pointed it out in the *New York Times,* "It is our nature to explore mystery, this is the way we are made." We do not sit comfortably in the presence of what we do not understand without trying to understand it a little better. This is our makeup; we're born that way. Children are inquisitive, curious; they're searching. We are born, therefore, to explore the boundaries of the universe. Long before men started trying to reach out there, people came out of their caves, so to speak, fashioned civilization, picked up telescopes, began peering through them, looking at the far-off galaxies swimming in the unlimited Atlantic of space. From the day people began looking out there, there has been a curiosity in us. What is it out there? It is our nature. We cannot eradicate that from us. It is to make an artificiality of our humanity to try to deny that we want to press against the boundary of existence. This is the way we were born; there is that much of God in us.

The other side of it, as Tom Wicker points out, is that we may perish in the attempt, but we're born with an insatiable desire to know, and we're born with the vulnerability of death. Here we are, not able to stop and not able not to die. What he did not say is, we need a Savior to bring these two together — the innate longing to know and the awful capacity to die. To know and to die, to blend these things into harmony is where we need, not a teacher, but a Savior.

We need a Savior to save us from greed. I have been but one little voice up and down this country talking to all kinds of people, talking about this matter of public corruption. It's just a refined form of mugging! A nice version of somebody hitting you across the head with a blackjack in a dark alley. It's the same thing. The most recent example is that the eleven people on our Board of Estimate in this city raised $9 million among them for their election or reelection. More than one-half of that $9 million was given by 175 people. Now they say that it doesn't buy them favors, but it buys them access. When anybody spends a million dollars for a job that pays $100,000 per year, he's either a saint, a fool, or he's already been made into a crook. Cut that apple any way you want; that's the only reasonable answer. We need a Savior to lead us out of our greed and our winking at corruption.

Nicodemus did not need a teacher; he needed a Savior. That's why he left his tomes, his parchments, and came by night looking for this wondrous guide. Jesus saw in his eyes that what he was talking about was not what his heart was saying: "Master, we know thou art a teacher." "Ah," said Jesus to him, "let's do away with those niceties, cut through the red tape. Let's get the trivial out of the way, Nicodemus. Except a man be born again — I'm not talking about teaching, reforming. You need regeneration. To be reborn, something has to happen in you. Never mind some more principles; you need God's Spirit that will guide your footsteps and direct your pathways. That's what you need." So Jesus did not spend any time in preliminary niceties. He went right to the heart of it, "Except a man be born again, he cannot see the kingdom of God." "Ah, how," said Nicodemus, still trying to rely on some human understanding, "Teacher, how can a man, when his bones are formed and fixed, how can he get back into his mother's womb?" "Ah," said Jesus, "he must be born again." The seeker wanted great mystery to fit into his little mind.

Well what does it mean? How shall I put it? What does being born again mean? Being born again means, hear me, impregnation with the Word and Spirit of God. Being born again means being ushered into a new life where flesh, with all it suggests, is no longer the definition of life. It is to be energized by the living Christ in a heart and mind ready and open and accessible, made ready by anxiety and by mistakes and by guilt and by shame, made ready for the Holy Spirit and for the Word of God. I'm talking about that Word which has life and power in it, that searches the heart, that roots out what is wrong. I am talking about the Word of God with a capital W, the Word of God that has power in it, strength, force, life and fire, grace and might. It must get in your heart, and there it fertilizes.

It gives a new birth, and such a soul is born again. The soul, the heart under conviction, realizes that something must be given up! A public confession is the declaration that the birth has occurred. Baptism is the symbolism that a change is going on. Born again, not "stillborn," but "begotten again unto a lively hope by the resurrection of Jesus Christ from the dead" (1 Peter 1:3). Search your soul; has it been delivered out of torment into peace? Such a one has already passed from death unto life. Such is the new birth, born again, born by the semen of the Word of God, energized and activated by the power of the Holy Spirit.

Entering the wounded heart, regenerating it, changing it, turning the soul all the way around — the word *metanoia* in the New Testament means "reversal, turn around, changed, made over, made new, a new creation." Our fathers used to say of the new birth, "I looked at my hands, and my hands looked new. Looked at my feet, and my feet looked new. Looked at the world, and the world did, too." To be born again is like a bird being loosed from a net and soaring up in the upper air with a glorious melody. Being born again is like a soul, parched and thirsty, coming to the everlasting fountains to drink from the inexhaustible waters of the living God. To be born again is to know that one has a crown of life that fades not away, to know that one has a new inheritance. The soul that has been born again may climb every snow-crowned mountain of the spirit, gaze upon every star of the faith, listen to the songs the angels sing, and know still that there is more beyond.